THE
WHITE GATE

Books by Mary Ellen Chase

A GOODLY HERITAGE
MARY PETERS
SILAS CROCKETT
DAWN IN LYONESSE
WINDSWEPT
JONATHAN FISHER: MAINE PARSON
THE BIBLE AND THE COMMON READER
THE PLUM TREE
etc.

MARY ELLEN CHASE

THE WHITE GATE

ADVENTURES IN THE
IMAGINATION OF A CHILD

Decorations by Nora S. Unwin

W · W · NORTON & COMPANY · INC · *New York*

The passage in Chapter 3 beginning "Our kitchen was large and sunny . . ." and ending ". . . this expression of righteous indignation," is reprinted, slightly altered, from *Recipe for a Magic Childhood*, New York, The Macmillan Company, 1952, with the kind permission of the publisher. This material first appeared as an article in the May 1951 issue of the *Ladies' Home Journal*. Copyright 1951. The Curtis Publishing Company.

Printed in the United States of America
By The Haddon Craftsmen, Scranton, Pa.

TO

LUCY TRUMAN ALDRICH

with love and admiration

CONTENTS

A PREFACE TO THE READER

THIS book has had a rather curious history, the relating of which may serve to define my purpose in writing it. The idea first came from the pleasant fortune of an article called "Recipe for a Magic Childhood," which I wrote for the May, 1951, issue of the *Ladies' Home Journal* and which described my early love of books in Maine during the late years of the last century. The article attracted sufficient favorable attention to justify its appearance as a small book a year later. Again it appealed to so many readers that my publishers suggested I write a story primarily for children which should deal with a Maine country childhood in the late eighteen-nineties. This during most of 1953 I tried to do, but with small success.

I finally reached the regretful conclusion that I was unable to write a book primarily for children. When I was a child, I did not know the difference between a book for a child and one for grown-ups. To me at nine or ten years old there was no marked contrast between *The Mill on the Floss* and *Five Little Peppers*. Both absorbed me equally, as did *The Old Curiosity Shop* and *Little Women*. It never once occurred to me that Phronsie Pepper and the March girls had been created for me, whereas Maggie Tulliver and Little Nell with their sorrows had been written for the understanding of my elders. If I did not understand Maggie and Little Nell and all that life had meted out to each, I at least loved and pitied them, which in a child is the beginning of understanding.

Once having admitted my defeat, however, I found myself still interested in writing of a childhood spent during those years which our complex life of today has made to seem so distant and so simple. I discovered also that what I really wanted to do was to try to recapture those vivid, if half-formed, impressions, those glimpses of reality and perceptions of wisdom, which in the long succession of dimly remembered days are in the life of a child like the flashing of fireflies in the darkness. For all of us as children, before we are beset and tossed about by the turbulence of adolescence, possess an instinctive capacity for wonder, for quick surprise, even for a puzzling sense of mystery, which redeems mere events in the beginning of our lives and which actually decides the wealth or the poverty of our later thoughts and, therefore, the nature of ourselves. These innate endowments, brightened or dulled by the circumstances of environment, inheritance, and training, weave by some secret, silent process strand by strand the spiritual pattern of our years and determine in no small degree the fabric of our lives. Nor is a child, in those early, fleeting apprehensions of the meanings latent within images, experiences, impressions, burdened by that anxious tyranny which all such meanings exact as the price of the mature imagination.

These chapters, then, have to do with adventures in the imagination of a child, adventures possible only through imagination, which in turn is nourished and nurtured by itself. They are not written for children except in so far as, mercifully, we never completely emerge from our childhood years.

Since "Recipe for a Magic Childhood" gave me the original idea and impulse for this much longer book, I have included in Chapter 3 a few of its paragraphs.

Mary Ellen Chase

Smith College,
April, 1954.

1

THE WHITE GATE

MANY years ago, when I was a child in Maine, our large and rambling white house was surrounded by a long white picket fence, which enclosed our apple orchard on one side and, on the other, set us apart from the field and apple orchard of our next-door neighbor. At the entrance to our driveway the fence was broken by a white gate, which swung inward or outward as necessary to allow for our comings-in or goings-out. The pickets of this gate were nailed firmly to sturdy cross-timbers, the lower one wide enough for us children to stand on, the upper one just high enough for our elbows or our fingers, depending on our ages. On either side stood a stout white post, that on the right holding the hinges of the gate and that on the left, its strong iron hook.

The most clear and lasting impressions of my childhood are related to this gate, which both sheltered and extended the small, tight world in which we lived. Behind it, our driveway moved past our house and toward the barn, also large and white, filled with the smells of hay and of kindly animals in their stalls and with the sound of pigeons, which swept in blue and white flocks to and from their dovecote high in the loft. Before it lay the country road, which ran downhill toward the village and the sea and uphill toward the sky. Dusty in the summer, muddy in the spring rains, cut into frozen ruts in the late autumn, and buried beneath snow in the winter, this road was, to me as a child standing on the white gate, next to the weather the most thrilling thing I knew.

If I looked behind me, there was the sureness of my home, a safety which lay warm and comfortable somewhere deep inside my pinafore. There was my bed with its bright patchwork quilts; there were my first books, my doll, my mother and father, my amusing grandmother, the warm kitchen with its black cookstove, the fire in the library, mugs of milk, and lamplight against the shadowy corners of our big rooms. But if I stared before me, beyond the pickets of the white gate, what excitement might not be coming or going along that road between the sky and the sea?

2

BEYOND THE GATE

TIM FINN, the blind man, might suddenly cut the bright space between the hilltop and the sky and come down the road, tap-tap-tapping with his stick, which told him where the road gave way to the deep ditch on either side. He was coming for his mail, which someone else must read for him, and for his food at the store, which somehow, my mother said, he could cook himself, though he could not see either the food or his pots and pans.

"Be polite to him," my father said. "Were it not for the Grace of God, you might be blind yourselves."

But in spite of the Grace of God, which we did not at all

understand, we were frightened of Tim Finn, especially of the black patch which he wore over his eyes and which made my brother Edward think darkly of pirates.

"Hush!" Edward would whisper from his place on the gate when the tapping came closer and the black patch was more clearly visible. "Be still. He can't see us, remember!"

Tim Finn usually tapped his way past us as we perched on the gate, red-cheeked and breathless from fear; but on one awful morning he stopped in front of us all. He raised his stick high in the air. He said:

"Do I, or do I not, smell the four Chase children on that gate?"

My sister Mildred, who was eleven when I was nine, was the only one of us who behaved well under these terrifying circumstances. She remained on the gate while my sister Edith, who was eight, and Edward, who was five, and I ran for the orchard and began to clamber each into an apple tree. She remembered even at that moment what she had often been told—that she, being the eldest, was *responsible* for the rest of us.

"Good morning, Mr. Tim Finn," she said politely, though her voice was small and weak. "Can we do anything for you?"

"No, my dear," said Tim Finn, beginning to tap the road again with his stick, "though I thank you kindly. There's nothing anyone can do for me but to pray that some day I'll see Our Lord face to face, for once He made the blind to see."

Edith, Edward, and I were too far up our trees at this moment to hear Tim Finn's odd request, but Mildred repeated it to us when we had at last come down and were on the gate once more. Before she told it, she exacted the promise of a penny from each of us (once each should have one to give to her) in return for *her* promise not to tell our mother of our rudeness. We were all puzzled by what the blind man had asked, for although we said our prayers every night, we were not used to people who spoke so openly about either prayers or Our Lord. Later on, after we had turned our pennies over to her and she had kept her promise, she asked our father about what Tim Finn had said. He explained that Tim Finn was an Irishman who had wandered into our village from God knew where in the days when he was not quite blind, and that he belonged to a church which was different from our own and used far different language. After that, I prayed for Tim Finn now and then, though I did not tell anyone, and I lost my fear of him, his black patch, and his tapping stick. Edward still believed him a pirate, whose eyes had been put out by his fellow pirates because he had discovered more gold than they on a desert island; and he also got the odd notion into his head that all Irishmen were pirates, though such a silly fancy was in no way my father's fault.

But Tim Finn was by no means the only source of excitement on our country road. Peddlers might and, indeed, did come down the hill once the road was dried of spring mud—dark women in queer, bright clothes with gold rings in their ears, who carried on their hips great oilcloth bags stuffed with household wares, trinkets, laces, shawls, and odd toys. These women came from far-off countries, Syria or Armenia, my father said, and we must always be kind to them as they were *footsore and weary* and *strangers in a strange land*. It was not difficult to be kind to them as we were rarely the losers by such behavior.

In early summer when school was over, the organ-grinder came either down the hill or up from the village. His name was Lorenzo. He said he had no other name. He ground out quick and merry tunes from his faded green organ, which he carried strapped around his shoulders, and introduced us quite formally each year to his monkey, Jock, who wore a green suit and a red hat with a green feather and shook hands with us all. My mother invited Lorenzo to come through the gate into the driveway, whereupon all the neighborhood children came running in from the board sidewalk outside our fence to dance in squealing circles through our orchard grass. When we presented our pennies to Jock, placing them in his small yellow hand, he took off his hat with a sweeping gesture and jumped to his master's shoulder or to the organ top between each offering. My mother gave Lorenzo a cup of coffee or a glass of lemonade before they went away; and Lorenzo never failed to remove his tattered straw hat and say, "Thank you, good madam," which impressed us deeply. Then with a strong shrug of his left shoulder which moved the heavy organ-strap nearer to his neck, he would set forth on his way, with Jock on his right shoulder and a crowd of us following, for his yearly coming was a mighty event in our lives.

Sometimes, but rarely, a cloud of dust at the top of the hill with a clatter of swaying pots and pans announced the dreaded but delightful advent of gypsies. Of all wayfarers on our road they were the most unwelcome, at least to all village parents, who hated their filthiness and feared them as thieves and, perhaps, even kidnappers. Once their dirty covered wagon and its approaching din were unmistakable, we fled in terror from the gate and up the driveway to inform our mother of their arrival, whereupon she quickly locked all our doors and allowed us only to peer with her from the front windows of our house. Down the hill their wagon rumbled and rocked, driven by a dark, evil-looking man with a black pipe in his mouth and drawn by tired, shaggy horses with faded red tassels above their ears. Two or three equally evil-looking dogs usually trotted beside it, and always barefoot, ragged children with long, untidy hair ran about in the dust. The terror which shook us all was wonderful as we saw from the window the iron pots swinging from beneath the wagon and watched the children performing rude antics in the road beside it. Once, the terror amounted to panic when the wagon halted and a small, slight gypsy woman in a long red dress and a red scarf over her head swung open the gate and came sidling up our driveway to the door. She was shaking a drumlike object surrounded by tiny bells, and she moved her feet gracefully in worn red carpet slippers as though in tune with the bells.

"Keep back!" my mother said to us in a hoarse whisper; but since at that awful moment she was too agitated to command our obedience, we slunk behind her to the dining-room window, which she opened before the gypsy woman had quite reached our porch.

"Go away!" she cried to the gypsy woman. "Go right away!"

The woman tossed her head then and laughed, showing even, white teeth against her dark face. And somehow her ringing, careless laughter there in our driveway made my mother seem, even in her fierce protection of us all, the loser in an odd battle between what was respectable and clean and safe and what was free and wild and exciting, even though dirty, shiftless, and dangerous.

"Your fortune, lady," the gypsy said in a high, whining voice, "for only a dime, dear lady. And don't be afraid, dear little ones. I've children of my own."

We stood transfixed at the open window, peering around my mother until the gypsy had laughed again and shaken her bells high in the air before she turned and danced down our driveway toward the waiting wagon and her filthy children by our white gate. Then they all laughed and screamed together, and one little boy about Edward's age put his thumb to his nose, waggled his fingers, and then turned a beautiful somersault in the dust, before the wagon creaked and clattered away down the road. I never forgot his rude gesture or the sight of his brown feet waving in the air.

My mother sank into a chair then, for her knees quite failed her, and we stood about her, safe but regretful. Danger was past, to be sure, but at what a loss!

"What's in their wagon?" Edward whispered, though how he dared to speak with my mother so unlike herself was a mystery.

"Dirt," she said briefly, now suddenly herself again. "Dirt and lice."

"What's lice?" Edward persisted, as we watched the disappearing cloud of dust.

"Something you will never know," my mother said.

Secretly we adored the coming of the gypsies, not only because of its immediate excitement, but because of the talk among our elders for days afterward, in the store, after church, and when callers came. Everyone always wondered why they chose to traverse our particular countryside, where cleanliness was the first of the cardinal virtues and where only the most outlying field or pasture could afford them a camping-place. We loved the thought of their fire at night with the children sprawling about it and some stew cooking in one of their iron pots, even more savory because it was made of stolen chickens or a stolen lamb. I loved, too, the odd knowledge, proffered by my father, that they wandered because they could not help it, because the necessity for wandering was placed inside them all when they were born and had lain inside them for centuries, *from generation to generation*, as he said. This idea was far more pleasing to me than my mother's almost angry opinion that they had taken to ranging about because their own faraway country could not tolerate their dirt and dishonesty, and so had most justly turned them out.

I used to ask myself in what far countries I would wander if only I had been made that way, and settled on several—Spain, and Italy, and California, and the Land of the Midnight Sun. And as I wandered, I wore a red dress, danced about with utmost grace, and swung a drum with tiny silver bells high into the air.

Indians often came down or up our road, usually singly and always on foot. These were mostly men, with small, long black eyes and high cheekbones; and since they were slung about with baskets and with long strands of withes, reeds, and grasses, sometimes plain but more often colored, they, too, lent brightness as well as excitement. Although they also were usually not overclean, they were not looked upon with the suspicion accorded to gypsies. My father insisted that they be made welcome because, he said, their race had been treated unjustly by our forefathers and we must make up for such injustice, late as it was to do so. Therefore, much to our delight, my mother always bought a basket from them for her sewing or for a Christmas gift. The scent of these baskets tantalized me since I could never, to my own satisfaction, discover its source. There seemed to be trailing arbutus (which we called *mayflowers*) in it, and apple blossoms, though clearly neither could have been woven into mere reeds and grass. Once, when I had the measles and lay in bed itching and burning, my mother allowed me to hold one of her baskets and smell it all I liked; and since it gave me great comfort and pleasure, I decided that in some strange way the Indians knew about things and even thoughts which would heal sickness and had somehow imprisoned these in strands of grass.

My father lent authority to this fancy by his confidence in the mysterious medicines which they sold, salves and ointments, and bottles of dark liquids with enticing names, Kickapoo Indian Sagwaw and Passamaquoddy Painkiller. He said that since they lived so close to Nature, they understood her secrets as we could not. This remark my mother treated with disdain, which mounted to scorn when my father claimed that both the Sagwaw and the Painkiller had cured him of many a cold and stomach upset. She said he knew very well that they were not concocted of innocent herbs and roots, and she always insisted that the bottles stand in a dark corner of one of our cellar shelves, away from the sight of anyone who might come in.

I would not give the impression that only foreigners, or *outlanders*, as our alien wayfarers were locally termed, lent drama to our road and to us children watching from the white gate. They were, of course, the unusual, the new, and the strange, and as such they severed the bonds and widened the boundaries of our snug existence; yet even in the ordinary and customary travelers on the road there was always interest for us. The scissors-grinder came two or three times a year, ringing his bell and calling out: "Bring out your knives and your scissors"; the meat peddler in his white-covered cart made his weekly round of calls, his joints and sides of beef and lamb and his wooden pails of livers and kidneys kept clean from the dust by the tight back doors on his wagon, which he opened when my mother came through the gate to inspect his wares; the fish peddler came, too, but except in the winter months when ice closed our harbor, we preferred to buy from the fish-boat, manned by Captain Andrew Cole, which moored at the town wharf three mornings each week and carried tubs of black-striped haddock at three cents a pound, clams and scallops at ten cents a quart, and, in the spring, alewives and tinker mackerel, which Captain Cole often threw in for goodwill only.

And always there was the passing up and down of our neighbors and our friends, bound for their mail or their groceries and stopping for some welcome words with us. There were laden hayracks drawn by slow, stumbling oxen; blue dumpcarts filled with straw-strewn manure for village gardens; and, in winter, sledges piled high with blocks of ice which, catching the sunlight, held quivering rainbows inside their pale blue transparency.

Even if there was nothing except the empty road itself, it never seemed empty to me. If I looked across it from the gate, there was a wide field with the wind tossing the grass, and beyond the field, tall trees and the white steeple of the church with its gilded weathercock. If I looked downward, there was the distant blue of the harbor water, coming from who knew where. If I looked upward, there was the top of the hill with the sky above and nothing beyond, at least nothing which I could see. I knew, of course, precisely what lay beyond, but I loved to pretend that I knew nothing at all—that the line of the horizon and the great half-circle of the sky above, blue, or gray with storm clouds, or red with sunset, held only mysteries quite unknown to me and waiting to be discovered in some strange time which people called the future.

3

WITHIN THE GATE

AT THE time when the white gate meant most to me, I was between nine and twelve years old, and those years lay between 1896 and the turn of the century. In those years on the coast of Maine there were no automobiles, almost no telephones, no gasoline engines, no electric lights, almost no bathrooms, or furnaces, or refrigerators, no running water, no boughten bread, no paper towels, no egg beaters, no soap flakes. In place of these amenities, which today make the running of a household comparatively easy, there were hard work in which all had a share, the comfortable knowledge of what one's days would be like, for they were usually very much the same, a sense of security impossible today, and plenty of time.

There was also the constant excitement of the weather. As today the lives of children are governed by school buses or car pools, the radio, records, comics, and movies, piano lessons and dancing school and mechanical toys, so our lives were almost completely governed by what the skies saw fit to bestow upon us.

I have been reassured of late by the conclusion of learned scientists that the weather, or the climate, as they put it, of certain portions of our country has without doubt undergone marked changes during the past half century. Since this has been evident to me for many years, I am relieved to know that my own conclusion has not been based on mere fancy. New England, where I have spent most of my life, today bears in terms of weather alone almost no likeness to New England around the year 1896. In spite of an infrequent blizzard, a hurricane, or even a tornado, by any one of which it seems to be declaring that it has not completely sacrificed its original nature, the weather has become a mild enemy, easily put to rout by central heating, plumbing, and municipal snowplows. In my childhood it was harsh, sinister, unpredictable, tyrannical; and, since it controlled our pastimes, the most exciting element in our lives.

Its tyranny over us was most evident, of course, in the winter; but in the year 1896 and for many years following, Maine winters claimed more than half the number of the months. Late September and all of October meant sharp frosts and early lamplight; November, high, biting winds and the first drifting snowflakes. From December until April, except for an occasional and brief January thaw, we were buried in snow, which lay three or four feet deep over fields and pastures and through which oxen, yoked to heavy sledges, plunged to their shoulders and men with shovels plowed to their hips in a fierce battle to break the roads. The mercury dropped to zero and below and remained there for days; the ice sealed our bay for seven miles out to sea and cracked with the sound of guns as the tide crept in and out beneath it; the timbers in our attics snapped at night; the air was cut by the blue, wavering breaths of muffled, venturesome people; children undressed by kitchen stoves or roaring fireplaces and, clasping hot flatirons or soapstones wrapped in cloths or in newspapers, dashed upstairs to huddle between blankets and under patchwork quilts in frigid rooms with tightly closed windows; families went to bed early in all houses, for every night someone had to get out of bed two or three times "to keep the fires up." When we went to school on bitter days (though in deference to the weather there was no primary or grammar school in January and February), bundled up in knitted hoods and heavy reefers, woolen mufflers and long black leggings, we carried hot baked potatoes in our mittened hands and kept these warm on the top of the schoolhouse stove against our return home. And whenever the weather allowed us to drive in our two-seated yellow pung behind our two black horses, we fondled these hot potatoes while my father in his bearskin coat and cap held the reins in his heavy fur gloves, and the sound of sleighbells cut the piercing air.

The white gate is never absent in my mind from the weather and especially from that of winter. There were few hours then when we could stand upon it, and often, after a heavy storm, it remained open for days, swung back upon its hinges and buried in snow except for the points of its pickets. My father, cutting the drifts of our driveway into great cubes with his shovel and hurling them right and left, was so worsted by the time he reached the gate that he welcomed an open space there through which he could more easily reach the road. But when there was less snow than usual or during a January thaw, he would close it again to limber up the hinges, he said, and keep it from warping too badly. On clear, bright mornings when it was closed, its pickets cast long blue shadows across the snowy road, making another gate there; and in the late afternoon as the sun went down, more shadows, now cold and gray, made yet another gate, this one extending inward toward our house.

The only day during the remainder of the year which held more fascination for us than any in the winter was the day in the spring which marked the shedding of our heavy underwear. No butterfly or moth swathed in a tight cocoon could have felt more exhilaration in bursting its bonds for its brief life in the sun and wind than we felt when, after hours of careful consideration, my mother decreed that our red-flannel combinations might at last give way to Ferris waists and cotton drawers.

It is impossible through mere words to do justice to this yearly ceremony. The rite was performed around noontime, for my mother waited cautiously to be sure the early warmth was not deceptive; but once she had decided that the hour had come, we tore upstairs and began to free ourselves while she divested Edward in the kitchen. The Ferris waists held buttons on tapes which met the buttonholes on the waistbands of our drawers, and we were so impatient for our imminent release that we found irritating the search for the exact meeting places of holes and buttons. But once we had managed the matching of these, the cool touch of cotton against our itching, sweating chests and legs, the intoxication of bare shoulders and arms to be covered only by a light frock, became the very essence of liberty itself, only to be increased when once the wind and the sun had had their chance at us. My mother hung our red flannels and our woolen petticoats on the clothesline for a good airing before they should be washed and put away against another autumn, while we tore about the orchard and finally came to rest on the lower timber of the gate. For there, with our legs and arms spread wide, we could feel the wind circulating through our cotton drawers and the warm sun getting beneath our percale, gingham, or calico.

This ritual, far more than freed brooks and blossoming trees, always to us ushered in the spring and summer. the blessings of which lay *beyond* the gate rather than *within* it. Beyond the gate lay the road, a summer highway in our imaginations. Through it we went with our pails for strawberries in a dozen meadows, for blueberries in rocky pastures, for blackberries in the tangled roadside thickets beyond the hilltop. We opened and closed it to play with our friends in their dooryards and fields, to set forth on Sunday-school picnics or on family drives, to lead our cow to pasture or our horses to the village watering trough. Within it, in spite of riotous summer games in our own field and orchard, lay autumn and winter and the secure sense of home and family, hard-won warmth, unending work, books, and lamplight.

My mother often used to say: "I'll be glad when winter comes. Then at least we'll know just where we are." Her remark arose, of course, from the comparatively harum-scarum ways of spring and summer, when relatives might visit us for a fortnight or more; when we all slept in sheets and wore cotton frocks, which meant mighty washings and endless ironings; when garden vegetables and wild berries were pickled or preserved against the winter shortage of food; when there were the August church sale and the Hancock County fair to cook for and cope with; when we children were always farther afield than she liked, forever begging for permission to go here and there and often forgetting our manners both at home and abroad; and when no one knew who might be coming at any hour on foot or by wagon up or down the road. In the winter all well-run country families were self-contained and almost constantly under their own rooftrees. In my mother's words, all knew precisely where they were; and I, for one, loved it.

Our household in the late eighteen-nineties was a large one, though not so large as it was destined to be several years later when Fate or Providence bestowed upon my parents four more children. My mother, in fact, distinguished herself by having her first baby at nineteen and her last at forty-six. Thus we were "well-spaced" children, but surely not by forethought or design. The spacing of families was a convenience undreamed of at that time when the phrase itself in its present sense was uncoined and when the methods of its assurance, at least in rural Maine, would have meant an unholy tampering with the mysterious Ways of God. When the first lot of us were young, our parents were young also, although we did not realize it. I can remember distinctly when I was seven confiding to a playmate of mine that my mother was twenty-eight years old, an age which seemed very old indeed to me.

When I was nine and first began to be aware of the security and the excitement of winter within our gate, our family consisted of my parents, my two sisters, my brother and me, my grandmother, who lived with us at least six months of every year, and our hired girl, who, since she came from just as good a family as ours, my father said, was a highly respected member of our own. She changed with the years, but I remember her best as Annie. She received two dollars a week and thought herself well paid. She always ate with us and entered into all our games and plays; and we helped her with the dishes, dusting, bedmaking, and other household chores.

Our family consisted, too, of several pet animals whom we knew better in the winter than in the summer when, like us, they ranged abroad more freely. As I look back upon these creatures, they seem to exist more clearly in my memory as the providers of dramatic moments than as playmates or companions. Our rat terrier, Ezekiel, has almost completely faded from my mind except for the day when, he being then a small puppy, my father cut off his tail so that he might look more as a rat terrier should. On that dreadful morning my sister Mildred burrowed beneath my grandmother's feather bed so that she might not hear Ezekiel's cries, even though the operation was done far away from our eyes and ears, and Ezekiel, my father said afterward, gave not so much as a yip. I remember my mother's bandaging the stump of his tail in the kitchen while we stood in an awed circle, seeing the stump grow plumper with strips of cotton and frightened into silence by my mother's tears. For we had never seen her cry before or known that she could, and the sight of her tears made a lasting impression upon me.

I have forgotten much, too, about our cat, Dolly Moses, except for her many kittens, always a sad problem, and for the truly alarming fits to which she was subject. Since these seizures occurred only in winter, they were perhaps the result of claustrophobia, for in the summer she caught flies daintily and slunk through the grass quite normally in search of field mice. But when her fits came upon her, she was terrifying, tearing round and round in circles, leaping on tables and chairs, and even running along the walls by some desperate power of balance. One day at dinnertime, a fit having overtaken her at just the moment when my father had lifted the cover from our large soup tureen to serve the clam chowder, she gave a frenzied leap for the table and fell into the tureen. The immediate effect of this monstrous act has never left my mind. It has nothing to do with the chaos of the table, with flying milk, bits of potato, and clams, or even with Dolly Moses struggling in the soup tureen. In comparison with a far more profound impression, these are all now as if they were not. What I remember is the instantaneous sight of the faces there, eyes widened, mouths opened, frozen into absolute stillness by horror. This fleeting glimpse, before the rescue of Dolly Moses, the cleaning up of the mess, and the laughter had begun, was a revelation to me, like my mother's tears over Ezekiel's stump. I had never known that faces could suddenly become so stricken and so still.

I suppose that we four children were very strictly brought up, at least in comparison with the rearing of most children today and perhaps even with other families of our generation. We always addressed our father as *Sir*, never daring to answer his questions merely by *Yes* and *No;* and in like manner we said *Yes, Ma'am* and *No, Ma'am* to my mother and grandmother. Needless to say, such courtesies were required whenever we addressed or responded to any person much older than we. Immediate obedience was the law of the household, arguments being not only discouraged but forbidden. We were early taught to listen to the conversation of our elders, into which we entered only when invited; but since invitations were frequently given, we did not by any means subsist in silence. We were early taught also to amuse ourselves and never allowed to "tease" either for attention or for entertainment. We were punished for disobedience, for rudeness, for marked neglect of our assigned chores, and for lying (at which exercise I especially showed early genius!), sometimes by being deprived of a coveted object or pleasure, sometimes, if the offense was particularly grievous, by a sound spanking either from a slipper or a whittled shingle and by whichever of our parents was on the spot at the moment. On the positive side of this perhaps relentless discipline, we were constantly reminded both by precept and example that the even running of our household depended upon the thoughtfulness of each for the other, that selfishness was not only wrong but unlovely, and that the respect and affection of our neighbors might be forfeited through the misbehavior of any one of us. Nor was generous praise ever withheld from us when we deserved it.

I have never felt a trace of resentment toward my early upbringing, which still seems to me just, if stern and unyielding. Two of my sisters, however, one from the first batch of children and the other from the second, disagree with me. They contend that we were needlessly controlled and repressed; and their contention has led, naturally enough, to a far different sort of training of their own children. Unmarried myself and, therefore, with no urgent personal stake in this matter, I have, nevertheless, been interested during the years in trying to discover what improvements either in methods or in offspring *they* have been able to achieve, given their own time and place. With the best will in the world, I can detect none, always provided, of course, that the bringing-up of children should result in a just measure of security and contentment during their childhood and in their being able later on to cope with life reasonably well and to find within it some enduring satisfactions for solace and enjoyment.

As I look back upon the four of us during those far-off days, we always seem a kind of corporate mass, since we were together referred to as *the children* and rarely, unless one of us was ill or injured, singled out for individual treatment or consideration. This impression, I suppose, lies in the fact that when we were directly under our rooftree, we behaved, with some daring variations, in much the same way, since that way was prescribed for us. We were, however, vastly dissimilar products and doubtless caused our parents hours of anxious discussion even although we were not aware of any such cogitations.

My sister Mildred at eleven was a quiet, tidy, capable

child, who could usually be depended upon to do what she was supposed to do. She was almost never punished, for she rarely got into trouble. She was diligent in school and excelled in sums, which talent delighted my father. She was often held up as an example to Edith and me, and she richly deserved that honor for she did everything with far more skill and care than did we. Edith at eight was the brightest of us all by every standard, and she was also by far the prettiest, with round, shining gray eyes and quick, graceful ways. She had an avid memory and could recite long poems, *The Psalm of Life*, *The Burial of Moses*, and many lines of *Hiawatha*, without a slip. She was merry and exuberant, adroit at making up games, and quite marvelous at mimicry. She and I should have shared equally in punishment; but she could assume a round-eyed innocence which had also a plaintive, even pathetic quality about it, most helpful in defeating justice. Both my sisters disapproved of me at nine, and, indeed, during all of my childhood. They said that I shirked my chores, was forever escaping to the toilet to read, made up untrue stories, and, except when I was under the scrutiny of my parents, "put on" in a disgraceful manner both in words and ways in order to draw attention to myself. All these accusations, as I knew even then, were entirely just. If my brother Edward at five possessed any distinct personality, it has been smothered in my memory. Since he was then the only son and had been waited for overlong, he was my father's idol and was early destined in my father's dreams for Bowdoin

College and, without doubt, for a Republican Presidency. I look back upon him mostly as a nuisance, in white frilled blouses and tight knee pants or kilts, whom we had to drag about when we played out-of-doors and tolerate within. I do remember that I loved to brush and comb his hair, parting it now on one side, now on the other, and plastering it down with soapy water. I recall, too, my father once saying, when he was displeased over my lack of industry or of co-operation, that since I showed no signs of rising any higher in life, I could doubtless someday support myself by hairdressing.

There were, of course, many days even in *our* winters when we were turned loose in the snowy fields where the pale blue sparkling crust would bear our weight and where we coasted down the slopes for hours with a wonderful sense of freedom. When the road outside the gate had been broken after a storm and pounded smooth by sledges and sleighs, we coasted down our long hill, going "belly-bump" on our sleds, a quarter-mile slide nearly to the village. We were often lucky enough at the foot of the hill, with only a brief wait, to get a ride back to the top on the empty sledge of some obliging farmer who had carried logs to the mill or ice to the town icehouse. The breath of his oxen coming back to us was sweet on the cold air, and the chips of pine, spruce, and balsam on the sledge boards smelled of the woods in the heat of summer.

Sometimes on bright, moonlit nights many of our neighbors, fathers and mothers as well as children, turned out for a community coast. For these thrilling descents fathers in turn steered long bobsleds, which had double runners, would carry eight or ten people, and went at really terrific speed from the top of the hill even to the town wharf, a distance of half a mile and more. And when winter was so relentless that the harbor ice froze for miles out to sea, men would map out a course upon it and hold horse racing there in their pungs and sleighs. Then good and fortunate children sat beside their fathers, glorying in the motion of the swaying sleighs, in the sharp ring of horseshoes upon ice, and in the hope of victory. Those were memorable occasions, talked of for weeks in anticipation and in retrospect; but for the most part winter, especially to young children, meant indoors and warm, fragrant kitchens.

Our kitchen was large and sunny with red geraniums in the eastern windows and from its western a wide view of fields and hills. Jutting from its south wall was our huge black wood stove, known by its name in raised iron letters across its oven door as *The Rising Sun;* and my mother kept it shining with a polish called by the same name. Between the eastern windows stood our kitchen table with a red-and-white checked cloth to match the geraniums, and by one of the windows was a Boston rocker, also painted red and flanked by four small red stools, which were pushed under the table when not in use. Our black iron kitchen sink separated the two western windows and held on its right shelf a green pump, which, when it wheezed and refused to work, had to be "caught" by a dipper of water drawn from the pail on the shelf to the left. My mother poured the water from the dipper held in her left hand slowly into the open top of the pump, while with her right hand she vigorously worked the handle until the water thus poured in mingled with that in the pipes below and caused it to issue in jets from the pump's nose.

Against the north wall of our kitchen, opposite the stove and affording a view from both eastern and western windows, was the piece of furniture which most intimately concerned us children. This was what we called the *secretary*. It was, in reality, a high and heavy chest of six drawers with two wide shelves above them. The upper shelf had on either side a stout carved post; the lower, below two smaller drawers, was just the right distance from the upper to serve as a perfect footrest for small feet.

My mother early saw in this old secretary an indispensable ally. Even in a kitchen as large as ours four pairs of feet about the floor could be not only an intolerable nuisance, but a possible source of perils to her and to us; and, while we were still very young, she had solved this problem by elevating us all to the top shelf of the secretary. A roller towel carefully placed below the armpits of the two children on the right and then around the convenient post, a similar securing of the two on the left, and we were proof against any cold drafts across our yellow painted floor, against kettles of hot fat, and, best of all, against the possible boredom of any number of January snowstorms.

We four spent innumerable winter mornings on the top

of that old secretary. I can still smell the warm spicy smells of gingersnaps baking in the oven, of apple pies rich with cinnamon, and of countless doughnuts merrily bobbing about on the surface of boiling lard. My mother sang hymns as she went about her work and encouraged us to sing with her. One of her favorites was *Shall We Gather at the River?* and all of us, joining in the chorus, loved to assure her that we most certainly would be there. "Yes, we'll gather at the river, the beautiful, the beautiful river," we would all shout together, each, I am sure, in those early days, thinking of that shining river only as some pleasant family picnicking ground on some pleasant, undefined day in the future. When the old clock in our dining-room slowly struck eleven, my mother reached up to each of us a fresh cooky and a cup of milk; and for this midmorning treat we laid aside our spool knitting-machines or the books we were reading.

It is always with books that the old secretary associates itself in my mind, for we read for hours there, sometimes the older of us aloud to the younger, sometimes, after we had all learned the magic of words, by ourselves. And we learned this magic early, not waiting to be taught at school. Without doubt, since we possessed a father who when at home was almost never without a book in his hand and a mother who somehow found time to read as well as to darn and cook, fashion clothes and refashion them, clean and wash and iron, we had absorbed the wholesome truth that books held manifold riches which we must discover for ourselves. There we would sit for hours upon our lofty perch while the snow fell or bitter winds blew across the white fields, not actually upon the secretary at all, but instead in Arabia with Aladdin or in the dark forest with Hansel and Gretel, with the four ingenious Robinsons on their mysterious island or with Oliver Twist in the workhouse, with David Copperfield on the Peggottys' houseboat, loving the alluring smell of crabs and lobsters and the nosegay of seaweed in the blue mug, or with Jim Hawkins crouching in the apple barrel of the *Hispaniola*.

My mother usually managed just after eleven to sit down for half an hour in the red rocking chair by the window. She called this half hour her *respite*, a word which early charmed me; and on days when no drafts were blowing across the floor (for even the Rising Sun was not always victorious over the worst of Maine weather), she would help us down from our Parnassus and allow us to sit upon our red stools while she herself read aloud to us. Here was the doorsill to complete enchantment, for she was seemingly as lost as we in whatever she was reading. The iron teakettle simmered on the Rising Sun; the red geraniums glowed with life; smells of our approaching dinner filled our noses, while my mother's voice brought trooping into our kitchen all those whom we admired or feared, loved or hated. Nor did she bring them among us only by her voice. She became as distressed as we over their misfortunes, as angry as we over their misdeeds. "Isn't he a wicked man?" she would cry when Fagin terrified Oliver in the loathsome garret; and, suiting her behavior to her disgust, she would slap the passage which chronicled such horrid goings-on. Then we must each in turn slap the page, she solemnly allowing us this expression of righteous indignation.

Those long winter days within our gate, when the drifting, silent snow dimmed our orchard and our field, or the cold without was sharp and frightening, or the early darkness crept over us, have never lived apart from books in my memory. Tied to the top of the secretary, lying by the open fire before our early bedtime, huddled into a ball under the square piano, dropping a hated dustcloth to draw Pip or Little Nell from the shelf, I laughed and cried; was lonely and even lovely; sat by gypsy fires; was born in a workhouse; met a convict by a grave in a dark, flat wilderness; died a dozen tragic and lamented deaths, my heart "mute and motionless forever." "When I die," I whispered to myself, picking up the hated dustcloth, "put me near something that has loved the light, and had the sky above it always."

4

MY UNCLES HEN AND HENERY, AND MY UNCLE ROSCOE

MY UNCLES Hen and Henery were not really my uncles at all, for neither my father nor my mother had brothers, and they had, therefore, deprived us of genuine uncles. Perhaps, indeed, this circumstance in the case of Uncle Hen and even more of Uncle Henery was a happy one since I could enjoy each to the full without those sometimes awkward burdens which actual blood relationship frequently places upon one.

Uncle Hen was the husband of my aunt Sa. They lived in a large white house but a short distance down the hill from our white gate, a house which, my father said, was far more beautiful than ours since it had white columns at its entrance, wainscot paneling, and over each door a carved white flower with leaves and tendrils. I never think of my uncle Hen in his home, though I am sure he stayed there often. Instead I always see him either at his woodpile, for he had a passion for sawing wood in his yard and for stacking it in neat and even cords, or in his shop, which stood some distance away in the field behind his house.

He was a carpenter by trade, and his shop, or at least the doorway of it, was one of the lodestones of my childhood. It was a small, gray, weathered building with a shingled roof painted red, four windows bordered by red casings, and double entrance doors also painted red; and it stood in some high grass of his field, which bordered our own. Why Uncle Hen never mowed the swath of grass around his shop was an untidy mystery to everyone. In common with the other men of the community he mowed his field carefully before July 4th, which was the deadline for haymaking, but he always left standing the grass directly next his shop. Some held the theory that he did not want to ruin his scythe blade with the bits of iron and ten-penny nails which the unmown grass might conceal; but I secretly believed that he felt more snug and secure with the tall grass surrounding him in his shop and that he also liked the sight of its ripening tufts and feathers swaying in the wind outside his windows.

Uncle Hen's shop was always in delightful confusion, in marked contrast to his house, which was always in perfect order. He had a long workbench on the east wall before his two eastern windows and another on the west wall before his two western windows; and he could move from one to the other as the sunlight moved. He had two sawhorses in the middle of the floor, and on the gray, worn boards of his walls he kept his tools, held in place by long nails or hanging from great rusted hooks. We never saw the actual floor of his shop for it was always hidden by shavings.

These shavings, made by quick, delicate movements of the bright blade of Uncle Hen's plane, are among the most vivid and satisfying images of my childhood. They fell from the yellow boards across his sawhorse in curls, or in tight whorls, or in long waving tendrils, and they rustled softly in the wind which blew through his open doors. I do not recall that we ever entered his shop, for we were never invited inside; but we stood for hours in the long grass before the doors, hearing the even scrape of his plane, watching the shavings take shape and fall, smelling the new, sharp fragrance of them in the air.

Uncle Hen was a small man as men go. He was stooped and thin and angular, and he gave the impression of being gray all over. His thin hair and side whiskers and mustache were gray, and his eyes when he looked at you and never seemingly saw you were dark gray like steel. He rarely spoke, at least in our hearing, and even as children we fancied that he lived in some odd world of his own, fashioned of fresh shavings, yellow boards with round brown knots in them, and tall unkempt grass. He rarely greeted us when he saw us standing before his open doors, though he never made us feel in the least unwelcome there. We were always consumed with curiosity as to what he was making, and occasionally this curiosity got the better of my sister Edith, who was not only of an inquisitive nature but had winning ways, so that her many questions were not irritating, like those of most children. When we had watched Uncle Hen saw carefully through black penciled lines, add to the shavings on his floor, carry smooth boards quietly to one of his workbenches, and fumble in the pockets of his gray denim apron for some nails or screws, Edith would bravely ask in the stillness, "What are you making now, Uncle Hen?"

He always took his time in answering her, and his reply was often difficult to hear because he had filled his mouth with nails, which always came out point first. His answers were brief and seldom varied much.

"Sa's got a notion for a table," or "Sa's hankerin' after a shelf."

But once on a warm summer day when the hot sunlight made the shavings more fragrant and we stood barefoot by the open doors in the grass, he gave a long answer, which for some unknown reason I have always remembered. On that day Uncle Hen had sawn three pieces of wood from a thin board into the shape of triangles, like large wedges of pie, and he had spent fully an hour carving the outer edge of each with his plane so delicately that the shavings from them were tiny wisps of curls. Then he had sandpapered them until they were smooth as satin. He kept holding each in turn up to the light, blowing on it, rubbing it between the palms of his hands. When Edith's curiosity overwhelmed her and she asked him politely what he was making now, he said (and clearly this time, for he had no nails in his mouth):

"Sa's set on a sort of wall-bracket. . . . For posies. . . . God knows why."

We never went to Uncle Hen's shop in the winter since the doors were never open then. But he did. In one corner to the right of the big red doors he had a small, rusted stove, and when on cold days we saw the smoke curling from a round stovepipe which cut the roof, we knew that he was there. Once when I came home alone from school, taking the path we had made for ourselves through the snowy fields from his shop to our driveway, I peered through one of the four windows and saw him sitting on a sawhorse before his stove. He was making nothing, just sitting there, and curling a long shaving around his forefinger.

I am sure that Uncle Hen like all carpenters shingled roofs, laid floors, and even built houses, but I do not remember him as engaged in these large, important occupations. My memory of him is associated always with objects, with things, with sounds and smells. These, stealing into my mind as a child, became at last endowed with their meanings, a strange and gracious process which is the miracle of memory and, indeed, of Life itself. When I think of my uncle Hen, I think of fragrant shavings curling from his plane, of high waving grass, of the sun streaming into his shop, and of us four children standing in its light before his doors, watching.

Uncle Hen, in spite of his laconic speech and his long silences, must have been the kindest of men; but kindness in itself means little to children unless it is marked by some outward and extremely visible sign. I do not think we ever connected Uncle Hen in our thoughts with kindness until one winter afternoon when he came to our house with such a sign, and even then the sign itself immediately ousted any gentle understanding of its origin.

My sister Edith was that winter for many weeks monstrously afflicted with boils, so that she not only had to sleep on her stomach but to spend most of the day in that position. Being a nervous, excitable child, she did not accept any misfortunes casually, and her boils had completely upset the usual even routine of our household. My mother spent hours in opening the boils, after the application of countless hot towels, a disgusting operation which I loved to watch, while Edith screamed in pain and protest.

Toward sunset one afternoon Uncle Hen came up the road and through our gate, now so set about by snow that its pickets and posts were barely visible above the shoveled piles. He carried in his hands a doll's bed, so perfect in every detail that my heart even now quickens at the thought of it. It was painted red. It had a headboard and a footboard curved like the pieces of Aunt Sa's wall-bracket. It had rounded spokes in a row on its sides, and little rockers which turned up at their four ends. And, most wonderful of all, on the top of each of its four posts was a tiny polished brass knob, which proved to be a bell and which rang when it was rocked.

My father and mother were as overcome as we children by Uncle Hen's gift. They made him place it himself by Edith's bed, and they said over and over again how kind he had been "to go to all that work" for her. As I recall it, my envious mind having been centered on the doll's bed and not on Uncle Hen or his kindness, he said nothing at all. I remember, however, that when he went homeward after his brief call, he did not return through the gate, but instead took our kitty-corner path which led through the banked snow toward his shop. Just as daylight was fading, we saw the smoke curling from his chimney and knew that he was sitting there by his rusty old stove.

Perhaps he had made the doll's bed for Edith because he had really liked her venturesome questions about the work of his hands.

II

I do not think that my uncle Henery was distinguished by his kindness to anyone; but he always held great excitement for us, perhaps because we were early aware that our parents discouraged too frequent companionship with him. He had nothing in common with Uncle Hen except for the fact that they were both Democrats. All Democrats were vastly irritating to my father since he was quite unable to understand how they could be decent, honest, and at least fairly intelligent and still hold such absurd opinions. It is but fair to say that most other men in our community and even in the entire State of Maine at that time agreed completely with my father.

But it was not only Uncle Henery's politics, mild at best, which annoyed my father. There were other traits in him which were thoroughly exasperating. He had no perceptible ambition, no profession or trade, and seemingly no aim in life but to enjoy himself and take no thought for the morrow. To allow others, in particular us four children, to enjoy his way of life with him did not in any way clear him in my father's eyes. He had no *gumption*, my father said. He was easygoing to the point of shiftlessness and, except for the thrift of his forefathers, would have been "on the town," a phrase which in my childhood described tersely the utmost depths of human degradation and failure.

My mother was not so much irritated by Uncle Henery as *distressed* over him and his ways. This word we sometimes overheard her say to my father and realized by her voice and expression that it meant deep sorrow and concern. She had reason to feel both, for Uncle Henery was married somewhat late in life to my aunt Do, who, although she was of no blood relationship, had lived in my mother's home when they both were girls and to whom my mother and, indeed, all of us were devoted. Aunt Do had married Uncle Henery when he was of middle age and she was but nineteen. Why she had done this was so unanswerable a question that it had ceased to be asked.

Uncle Henery and Aunt Do lived in a large red-brick house nearly a mile from our own and beyond a grass-grown driveway bordered by ill-kept cedar trees. The house had been built many years before by some earlier member of Uncle Henery's careful, ambitious, and thrifty family, which he had disgracefully allowed to run to seed, my father said, just as he was now allowing the house to run to wrack and ruin. We were conscious of neither wrack nor ruin, when we went to spend the day there, a permission granted us two or three times a year. We thought their house far more delightful than our own since no restrictions were placed upon our use of it. We could race pell-mell through all its many rooms, slide down the steep banister of its staircase, find any number of treasures in its barn, and, best of all, in summer explore the shoreline below its orchard. Uncle Henery usually pottered about the beach there, baling out his several waterlogged boats or occasionally, after one was dried out, painting her and asking our advice as to what he should name her. My grandmother once said in a moment of irritation like my father's that Aunt Do and Uncle Henery lived on *love and green wood*, a description which puzzled us since the first means of sustenance was beyond our understanding and since Uncle Henery heartily disliked the sawing of wood, green or dry, and rarely, if ever, piled it in regular, beautiful piles as did Uncle Hen.

Uncle Henery was a tall, thin man with a completely bald head which was always red like his face. His eyes were the most extraordinary thing about him. They were large and round like perfect circles and of such a startling blue that one never forgot them. The rest of his face meant nothing at all except for its redness, which was generally conceded to be the result of intemperance. He loved the sea which, when its tides were high, stole up nearly to his orchard trees, and, when its tides were low, allowed him to admire his boats, for most of these were so firmly embedded in mud and flats that they were not visible at high water. The deepest regret of his rather long life was that he had not gone to sea as a boy, but this was one of the many things he had never got around to. I think the reason we loved to spend hours on the beach with Uncle Henery was his easy way of doing things with no fuss or worry or the least sense of the passage of time. This made us feel rested and relaxed as we rarely were allowed to feel at home.

Although tradition said that Uncle Henery had once run a store, he held, so far as *my* memory serves me, a regular job only once during my childhood. Shortly after Mr. Grover Cleveland again became President of the United States, in 1893, and my father said our country was also, and again, going to wrack and ruin, Uncle Henery became postmaster for four years. I was six years old then and ten when he retired happily to the beach; but I remember vividly how blue his eyes were as he greeted people gaily through the little window when they came to get their mail. People complained that he sometimes forgot to order stamps and postcards in time and thus delayed all village correspondence abroad and that to fill out and purchase a money order at his disheveled desk within the office was the most irritating of ordeals; but perhaps such criticisms were natural enough in a community so overwhelmingly Republican as our own. At all events, I loved to go for the mail and see his round blue eyes and his red face framed in his window.

Just as my uncle Hen was consumed by a passion for sawing wood either to burn or to fashion into a wall-bracket for posies or into a doll's bed, so my uncle Henery, to whom all Uncle Hen's passions were clearly distasteful, was consumed by one of his own. Half a century before newspapers and magazines began to urge people to *increase their word power by learning a new word each day*, Uncle Henery had conceived this idea on his own. I do not think he was a born reader, his excursions into print being limited to the weekly county paper, called *The Ellsworth American*, and *The Farmer's Almanac;* but he loved a dictionary. He kept a worn old Noah Webster under the kitchen table and spent hours conning its pages, sitting by the table and writing down the words which most appealed to him on a school tablet with the blunt stub of a pencil. Small, neat words held no charm for him, for as I understand now, he was a large-minded man in certain odd ways, and he loved mass and volume in his vocabulary.

I do not think Aunt Do appreciated Uncle Henery's skill with words any more than she welcomed him and Noah Webster at her kitchen table while she was trying to do her housework; but we loved it. On those rare summer afternoons when we were allowed to be with him on his topsy-turvy beach, I listened with expectation and awe to whatever unfamiliar word he might dislodge from his pleasant, rather loose mouth and his somewhat scattered teeth. He called his waterlogged, unseaworthy dories and skiffs his *flotilla*, or *armada*, or *argosy;* and since he always laughed slyly as he did so, he made quite evident, as I see now, his good-humored agreement with everyone else that his boats, his words, even his way of life were all a joke, or a jest, or a laughingstock, but never a bitter one to him. Whenever the tide had cast up some scraps of driftwood, or, better still, some rope, he would say it was a *bountiful* tide, or a *magnanimous* tide, words which I tried hard to remember, but too often lost, and longed to hear again. Sometimes he coined words of his own. The summer following my sister Edith's siege with boils, which had left her very thin and scrawny but more lively than ever, Uncle Henery, as he anxiously watched her skipping from rock to rock, said that she was *emaciated by energitis*. This captivating phrase we carried home among the four of us, saying it over and over so as not to lose it as we ran giggling through the village and up our hill in that reckless abandon which always marked our return from Uncle Henery's. We were disappointed at my mother's reception of it.

My father often said in not too pleasant a manner that whatever money Uncle Henery's respectable and thrifty forebears had left behind them could not last forever. Occasionally Uncle Henery himself became aware of this disturbing truth and began to set and haul some lobster traps.

He did not make these himself, for he said it was *superfluous* labor. During a morning's pleasant row in his least leaky dory, he said, he could *salvage* all he needed from the ledges and islands of the outer bay and repair them at his leisure. When the wind blew from the northwest, he did not even need to row. Instead, he raised a large umbrella, which he held in one hand from his seat in the stern of the dory, and with the tiller in the other skimmed serenely out to sea.

Uncle Henery always called lobsters *crustaceans*, just as he spoke of clams, which he did not enjoy digging, as *mollusks*. I shall never forget the momentous occasion on which I first heard the former of these terms. My father being away for a week and my mother always more lenient with us when he was not at home, we were allowed to play on Uncle Henery's beach. When we got there, he was in his hip boots at the mooring of his dory, slowly baling sea water from between her thwarts. "Ahoy, there!" he called, for, having been by his nature deprived of going to sea as a young man, he favored sea terms. "Who cares to plumb the mighty deep for crustaceans?" My sister Mildred declined at once, not only for herself but for Edward, who howled in useless fury. Since she was older than we and perhaps already had a less romantic, or surely more realistic, view of Uncle Henery, she tried to decline for Edith and me also, but together we resisted her. Uncle Henery obligingly hauled the dory inshore, and with his help we were soon seated in the stern while he prepared to row amidships.

This adventure being truly momentous and never repeated, I should remember it in every detail, but the simple truth is that I remember little, or nothing at all. The dory must have pitched about as dories always do in trap-hauling; we must have been terrified and wet to the skin; we obviously returned in safety. But all these certain details have completely faded from my mind. Nothing, indeed, has remained there but the words of Uncle Henery's salutation, our frenzied embarkation, and two round blue eyes which continue to stare innocently at me and which are still quite apart from Uncle Henery's face, or his oars, or even from any *crustaceans* which we may well have *plumbed from the mighty deep.*

III

My uncle Roscoe commands, even deserves, less importance than my uncles Hen and Henery, for my memory of him is far less vivid than of them. Still it would be a pity to neglect him entirely, for the one odd anxiety which seemingly governed his life made a sharp and lasting impression on me as a child.

This anxiety of Uncle Roscoe's amounted, as I now understand, to an obsession since it was the result of frustration; and although these now familiar terms were rarely heard fifty years ago, the difficulties they refer to presumably existed in fact, if not in conversation, and wrought their uneasy consequences then as now. Except for his peculiar obsession, I do not recall many things about Uncle Roscoe;

but the memory of those frets and worries which so often upset him still illuminates my imagination.

Uncle Roscoe lived with my aunt Cad, his wife, in that half of the paneled white house which was not occupied by Uncle Hen and Aunt Sa, and, like them, neither he nor my aunt Cad was bound to us by ties of close blood relationship. He was a paper hanger, and from his means of livelihood arose the source of his distress, which at times increased to anguish. Uncle Roscoe feared and hated roses, not in gardens or climbing over trellises, but on wallpaper. He deplored, it is true, all other flowers on wallpaper, but roses depressed him beyond words. The very thought of them there on certain of the tight rolls of sample wallpaper which he brought to his patrons for their inspection and choice plunged him into depths of despair.

The reason for this suffering lay in the fact that Uncle Roscoe was an idealist about his job. He was, in other words, dedicated to the perfect matching of long strips of wallpaper; and the frequent periods of gloom which were his lot in life had their sources in the past over which he had no control whatsoever. Most of the houses in our village were old, and in the course of years they had either "settled" or even swerved a bit from their original solid foundations. These stealthy movements, for which only time could be blamed, had resulted often in uneven walls which defied even Uncle Roscoe's care and skill, especially if someone demanded roses upon them. Stripes were perilous enough, for they often slanted in spite of all that he could do; but roses, whether large and single, or in bunches, with their stalks and leaves, quietly thwarted all Uncle Roscoe's dreams of perfection. He wanted plain wallpapers, or at least those with little design, and always strongly advised them.

As a child, I did not, of course, understand fully the painful reality of Uncle Roscoe's frustration; and I have often wondered why it remains the one thing in my mind entirely clear about him. I suspect it has stayed there through all these years because my first apprehension of it was connected with pain and shame. For the most tenacious memories and images of children are often lodged within their consciousness as the result of disquieting emotions of one sort or another. I had gone one morning to spend an hour with my aunt Cad; and while I was paring and slicing some apples for her to make a Brown Betty for Uncle Roscoe's dinner, I cut myself badly between the thumb and forefinger of my left hand. Aunt Cad rushed for the bottle of iodine and poured a generous quantity into my cut, which not only increased my pain to agony, but also resulted in my disgracing myself by being sick on her clean kitchen floor. In the midst of this confusion and my awful embarrassment Uncle Roscoe appeared early from his work and slumped disconsolately into his chair by the kitchen table. He gave me and my plight not so much as a glance. He merely said, "My God! More roses!" and buried his face in his hands.

My aunt Cad was so shocked by his profanity, which was really a desperate cry for help, that when she led me home, she explained fully to me how roses *always* upset Uncle Roscoe and how the unfortunate choice of them by Miss Sarah Bent for her sitting-room walls had been the cause of his unseemly language in my presence. She talked to me almost as though I were her own age, perhaps to give me back my confidence and self-respect, for I was still crying from sickness and disgrace. She told me that Uncle Roscoe was, of course, silly about the roses, but that we all had our own secret burdens as I would understand when I was older.

I never forgot this incident or, apparently, her explanation, so that later, whenever I saw roses on any of our neighbors' walls, I was again back in Aunt Cad's kitchen with my pain and shame and with Uncle Roscoe's dreadful knowledge that he must endure a far greater portion of both. Indeed, I think that I was more aware than even my mother herself of the cloud under which he lived and worked. For when I was some years older and my mother insisted on roses for one of our bedroom walls, Uncle Roscoe's petulant comment, "They're your own risk, remember," seemed to her only fussy and, as she said, stubborn. But I knew better.

5

MY AUNTS DO AND MI

MY AUNT Do's real name was Elizabeth, but we never called her that. We called her simply Do, pronouncing her name like that of the female deer rather than like the verb of action, and omitting the *aunt*. The source of this odd address I have long since forgotten, if I ever knew it.

She was, as I have said, the wife of my uncle Henery; but in some singular way, which I felt even as a child, she seemed quite separate from him. My aunts Sa and Cad quite clearly lived to make the ways and paths of Uncle Hen and Uncle Roscoe, in so far as they could, ways of pleasantness and paths of peace, except that my aunt Cad, who was a deeply religious woman, lived also for God. Like them Do was an excellent housekeeper and cook, and she never for an instant neglected Uncle Henery's actual needs. But once those were attended to, and even while she was attending to them, she lived her own life. Perhaps this emancipation of Do's at a time when most wives and husbands were seemingly bound closely to one another, was an act of *adjustment*, or of *security*, or even a *necessity for survival*, terms then rarely, if ever used, and, had they been in use, quite meaningless to a child. I simply knew that Do was Do, that Uncle Henery was Uncle Henery, and that that was that.

Do was a tall, handsome young woman with eyes almost as blue as those of Uncle Henery, but with none of the vagueness of his. Hers sparkled with merriment, which I do not think she could often have felt since her life clearly had its difficulties and trials. I am sure that we four children afforded her some measure of compensation for these, as she was often at our house sewing with my mother and doing all manner of pleasant things for us. In those days, when shawls were an indispensable part of a woman's wardrobe, she wore a very long light-gray one with fringe. When she came to our house on winter days, we used to see her coming up the road and through our gate with her shawl held closely about her, swathing her from shoulders to feet. Over her head she wore a pale blue "fascinator," knitted by herself, which covered her hair, closely surrounded her rather plump cheeks, and met the shawl at the back of her neck.

Do came to our house always in the afternoon since she was busy during the morning not only with her housework, but with her knitting-machine. In common with many other rural Maine women of her day she earned money (which she sorely needed) by running a knitting-machine. This intricate contraption was attached by iron bars to her dining-room wall near her windows facing the sea; and she worked it by moving rows of tiny steel needles back and forth after she had tampered with them in some mysterious way with a steel hook. Skeins of wool on either side of this machine were thus converted into long black stockings, or into men's heavy white or gray socks, which she sold to some firm in Boston, which thereupon sold them elsewhere at a much higher price than she received for her work. I loved to watch her manipulating this machine, which she said was easy to do, but which seemed most complicated to me.

On the afternoons when she came to our house, she usually brought us surprises beneath her gray shawl. These were always things that she had made for us, gingerbread men, or cookies, or little decorated cakes, or clothes for our dolls and, perhaps, some knitted horse-reins for Edward. Sometimes she brought no presents, but, instead, once she had taken off her shawl and fascinator, announced that her surprise was an invitation to spend a day with her. This always sent us into a paroxysm of excitement, for, as I have said, we adored those rare days at her and Uncle Henery's house.

I am grateful to Do for many blessings, some of which I have related elsewhere; [1] but I always see her most clearly as one of the actors in my first real play, or drama, for I was the chief actor therein, being called upon without warning to enact a role which I had until then not known existed. The first act of this drama took place in our dining-room between eight-thirty and nine o'clock in the evening of the 23rd day of February, in the year 1896. This date and hour marked the eve of my ninth birthday, a day which I was that year to spend in bed from some illness, the nature of which I have forgotten.

Since unheated bedrooms were always a problem in case of illness, my mother moved a trundle bed into the dining-room when but one of us was ailing, reserving our two front rooms for more general casualties like measles, mumps, or whooping cough; and on that February evening I was in bed in a corner of the dining-room and presumably asleep. I had, in fact, been sound asleep ever since the supper things had been cleared away and my sisters and brother had gone to bed in their cold rooms upstairs. But around half past eight I became suddenly conscious of whispered conversation going on at the dining-room table. Peeking out from my covers, I saw my mother and Do sewing there by the light of our large table lamp, and from the strange

[1] In *A Goodly Heritage*, Henry Holt and Company, 1932. There is a chapter also in that book about my aunt Cad, there called by her real name, Caroline.

presence of my doll and her cradle on the top of the table, I suspected that they were making something for her and for me.

I closed my eyes tight, lay perfectly still, and listened, since I did not dare longer to look. They were saying in whispers, with soft, low laughs now and then, how surprised and happy I would be when I should awake in the morning to find by my bed my doll, sick, too, in a new nightgown, in her cradle with a new sheet and patchwork quilt. And as they whispered on, I knew that they were fashioning these things for my birthday.

I was tense from two emotions as I lay there, emotions so real that I have never forgotten them. The first was an almost guilty terror lest they should discover I was awake when I should have been fast asleep and reprove me as for some misbehavior. But the second, when it seized me, was so much stronger than the first that, after a few breathless moments of fear, it quite ousted the first from my imagination. What really tormented me as I lay there was the necessity of guarding my mother and Do from the knowledge that I was aware of their secret. For I suddenly realized as I listened to them whispering and laughing together, in the lamplight, by the table, that older people sometimes had secrets also, which they held sacred as did children. In a strange way, too, on that evening when I was just leaving eight for nine years old, I understood that older people might be children also. My mother and Do had always before seemed old to me, but as I lay there listening,

I knew all at once that they were also young and that I must protect them from disappointment and regret, guard their secret, preserve their happiness from ruin.

This new act of pretense was, I understood too, entirely different from all the pretending which I had known before. If I pretended that I was covered with leaves like the Babes in the Wood, or that I was Maggie Tulliver with the gypsies, or Little Nell lying dead while her canary still stirred in its cage, no one but me was in the least affected; or if I pretended that I was innocent of some misbehavior when I was guilty, I alone bore the punishment. Here, in this new play, others were clearly concerned, their comfort, their pleasure, their sense of safety. I could not realize then those countless necessities for such pretense which the years would bring, those half-truths and evasions and concealments required of one in order that the hopes and dreams of others may be spared; but I feel sure that I had a glimpse of them as I lay that night in my trundle bed and desperately pretended to be asleep.

When the dining-room clock struck nine and my resources for play-acting were fast wearing out, I knew that the act was mercifully drawing to its close. Do tiptoed to the hall to fetch her shawl and fascinator and with a last delighted laugh whispered goodnight to my mother. I lay completely still while my mother tucked the bedclothes more tightly around me and made sure I was warm and fast asleep. The last thing she did before she closed the draft of the stove and lowered the wick of the lamp was to place my doll in her cradle beside my bed.

Perhaps the first act of this play so depleted my powers that it stole all memories of the second, presumably performed in the morning when I discovered my birthday present and expressed my complete surprise and delight. For of that I remember nothing at all.

II

My aunt Mi differed from my other so-called "aunts" in being, I often thought, *unfortunately* bound to me by ties of blood relationship, for I liked her the least of them; in fact, neither I nor any of us liked her at all. Still, there she was, old, querulous, fussy, and demanding, bone of our bone and flesh of our flesh, and we had to put up with her. I must say in fairness to Aunt Mi that she did not often exact the costly price of our tolerance and charity; but the rare occasions when she did are stamped indelibly upon my memory.

She was (if I have our family tree straight after all these years) an aunt of my mother's, and, therefore, our great-aunt. Her real name was Almira, although she was never called by it, and her maiden name had been Hinckley, a surname widely, well, and favorably known in our community. She had been married once upon a time to a man named Scammon, who came "from away" and whom we had never known, save to pity. Since his death, for he presumably had died, she lived with some forbearing relatives in an outlying district some five miles distant from our home.

On her infrequent visits to the village Aunt Mi spent a few days with her sister, Miss Lizzie Hinckley, also old and querulous, who "kept" for a time our Ladies' Social Library in one room of her beautiful old house. Her house, much extended and remodeled, is now the Blue Hill Memorial Hospital; and I never enter its front door facing the sea but that I am again in the room on the left of the entrance as it used to be when it housed the Ladies' Social Library, open one afternoon and one evening a week throughout the year. This name in Miss Lizzie's day (we never called her *aunt*), was a misnomer, for not only was the library skimpy in the extreme, but it was hardly *social* with Miss Lizzie in charge and with Aunt Mi occasionally in the warmest corner next the stove.

Miss Lizzie wore eyeglasses, which quivered constantly, and a black "hug-me-tight" over her black dress. She sat bolt upright at a table with a large blank-book upon which she entered books returned or withdrawn. She was very thin and of a pale blue color, with cold, pale eyes. I remember once, when I asked her feebly for *Twenty Thousand Leagues under the Sea*, she tried to give me *The Wide, Wide World* instead, as "better for you." I had read *The Wide, Wide World* several times for want of more nourishing fare, although I did not like it overmuch, and I politely declined her suggestion. Luckily, for her, *Twenty Thousand Leagues* was out, so that I left with nothing but relief.

At those times, usually in the winter, when Aunt Mi visited Miss Lizzie and increased the depression of the Ladies' Social Library, she always came either for dinner with us or to spend the night. When she chose to come for dinner, my father said she was *the destruction that wasteth at noonday;* when she came for overnight, he called her *the pestilence that walketh in darkness.* Although he made these remarks to my mother, the older of us knew quite well what he meant, since we had to memorize psalms early both in school and Sunday school; and though the humor and aptness of his comments were doubtless lost upon us then, they have remained a cheering legacy.

Aunt Mi was small, thin, and pale blue like her sister; and she was always cold. Her hair was very thin also, crimped in front and of a yellowish hue, probably the result of overhot curling tongs. I do not now recall much about her dinners with us except that they were distinctly subdued meals given over mostly to Aunt Mi's catalogue of all the things which were wrong with her: her digestion (though she ate extremely well); her existence far from the center of things; her rheumatism; her lack of children; her fading bank account; and the *cold.* I do remember, however, with complete clarity her nights with us, largely, I suppose, because at least one of them filled me with a haunting dread which lasted long after Aunt Mi had returned to her isolated existence, far from the center.

Aunt Mi always spent her one night with us in a small bedroom off our dining-room. This room was not only the warmest bedroom in the house, but, since it demanded no stairs, coddled her rheumatism. The preparation for her retiring began early, for she insisted upon hot rocks in her bed. A soapstone was far too heavy and unwieldy, she said, and a flatiron was little better than nothing since it had to be moved so often from place to place. Moreover, in her opinion, rocks, if thoroughly heated, held their warmth longest.

The rocks were not hard to find even if there was snow when she came, as there usually was, since there were plenty of them under our barn, left there, I suppose, years ago when the foundations were laid. Aunt Mi had to have six sizable ones, and these had to be well heated in my mother's oven for some hours before bedtime. My mother's face as she moved Aunt Mi's rocks to make room for Johnny-cake, pot roast, or potatoes, revealed her state of mind, though unlike my father she used no words to describe it.

At precisely eight o'clock, which was Aunt Mi's bedtime, the six rocks, done up in pieces of old blankets, were placed in her bed, two at the foot, and two on either side, in the proximity of her hips and shoulders. Then a lighted lamp was placed on her bureau; and after a doleful goodnight to all and the prophecy that the cold was steadily increasing, Aunt Mi went to her room. How she managed to circumvent the rocks on the outside of her bed, I do not know, but she did; and, once within it, she called to someone to blow out her lamp.

I suppose it must have been in the discharge of this duty

that I once saw her in bed and felt creeping over me the terror which this sight engendered; or I may have gone into her room with my mother. At all events, I saw her there. She wore a tight black woolen cap over her head, and as I looked upon her among her hot rocks, her blue, shrunken face against the white pillow, even more shrunken because her teeth were out and in a saucer on her stand by the bed, I was overwhelmed, stricken by a sudden and dreadful understanding.

I knew, of course, with the unfamiliar, remote, unreal acquiescence of childhood, that everyone must sometime grow old; but the recognition, the cruel confirmation of this certainty, had never before wrapped me in its chill. Someday, I realized standing there in Aunt Mi's shadowy room, after long years had passed, to be sure, but *someday*, I, too, would be old. I do not think I saw myself as Aunt Mi, wizened, and unwanted, and disliked. Those were minor fears, lost in this strange new burden of time, this stealthy creeping on of days, against which no one, try as one might, could do anything at all.

6

LANTERNS

THE instantaneous burst of electric light which to-day transforms darkness to radiance never ceases to give me wonder. I virtually never produce it with a turn or pressure of my thumb and forefinger that I am not back again for a moment in our kitchen on the morning of any day in my childhood. I am standing there at our kitchen table and watching, or helping with, the chore of cleaning and filling our many lamps.

This inevitable task entailed, first, the spreading of news-papers on the table and, next, the gathering of "lamp cloths" from the isolated hooks where they were kept, well away from the danger of fire. This done, the lamps were assembled from chandeliers, wall-brackets, shelves, and bedside stands. Then began the gentle removal of soot from wicks, the even trimming of them with scissors when necessary, and the insertion of new ones; the wiping of oily globes of glass or metal; the washing in hot soapsuds of fragile chimneys, and perhaps of porcelain shades, and the polishing of them; the careful refilling of the globes with kerosene poured from a tin can with a bright red spout; and, finally, the cautious carrying of the lamps back to their appointed places. Since this delicate, if disagreeable, job required both skill and prudence, it was rarely entrusted to children under twelve or thirteen.

The cleaning of lanterns, however, exacted less competence, and we were trained for more advanced work by our trimming and filling of these. They were made of tin with an ill-smelling base which held the oil. From this base rose two curved rods which perforated a tin top and joined above it to form a handle. The chimney of rather thick glass screwed into a groove in the base and could be extracted for cleaning and then replaced without much difficulty.

In our household we had three lanterns in constant use during the hours of darkness. One, which hung above our front door, was lighted at nightfall and put out at my parents' bedtime; another was the barn lantern, the largest of the three, which my father used when he milked our cow on autumn and winter mornings and evenings and did his other chores there; and the third was the lantern which burned all night on the kitchen table for light when someone must get out of bed to keep up the fires in winter or when any nocturnal excursions abroad became necessary. One of these excursions was our bedtime dash to the toilet.

My father often reminded us, when on bitter nights we deplored the necessity for this journey, of our great good fortune in having our toilet located in the barn instead of discreetly hidden behind shrubbery at some distance from the house as was the case with several of our neighbors' conveniences. He said that we did not sufficiently appreciate this distinction; and I must admit that in zero weather the distinction did not assume the qualities of any marked differences in discomfort. Roofless cold in hurried transit might be a trifle more piercing than roofed; but the contrast was not so obvious as to exact any substantial measure of gratitude.

Our toilet, or *privy*, the term most commonly used, was situated beyond the kitchen, beyond a long woodshed, beyond the barn proper, and at the end of a long passageway which shut off its approach and entrance from the barn floor. Its outer wall faced the weather and its inner separated it from the first of the row of stalls occupied by our horses and our cow. When we set forth for it at bedtime, my sister Mildred led the line of us with the lantern in her hand.

Although this nightly procession at the time held little or no humor for me, I have often laughed in retrospect over it, and especially over our paraphernalia designed for it. One

Christmas at about my eighth or ninth year my aunt Do had given each of us a quilted toilet seat. She had made these of bright patterns of calico and padded them with cotton batting; and she had also taken the trouble to outline the name of the owner in red letters on a generous piece of white cloth, stitched to the finished product. We were vastly pleased with her gifts since they were not only a protection against the cold, but also an exciting innovation. We always heated them over the hot kitchen stove before we started on our way, and then we stuck our heads through the holes to feel the warmth and comfort on our shoulders.

It was not the toilet seats, however, which impressed themselves upon my memory so much as the lantern light in our barn. When we reached our destination, the lantern was hung on a nail just outside the door of the privy; and as we waited our turns at entrance, it lighted dimly the great barn, casting long shadows on rafters and walls. I have never forgotten those shadows there, or the smell of hay and of warm breaths penetrating the cold, or the stirring about of the horses in their stalls, their snortings and snufflings, or the way they turned their heads to fix solemn eyes upon us, or the white mist coming from their nostrils and just visible in the dim light. Sometimes, as I waited in the half-darkness, I put my hand on the nose of Lady, who, because she was a Morgan mare and much prized by my father, had a box stall to herself; and I always felt a sense of wonder at the warmth of her soft skin on the coldest of nights.

The barn in lantern light was never a frightening place

to me. With its tightly closed doors against the cold and its loft crammed with hay, it seemed instead safe and secure in spite of its shadowy corners and its great gulfs of blackness which the rays of the lantern could not pierce; and I felt an odd kinship with the creatures there who, I imagined, returned my feeling and welcomed our brief entrance into their long, dark night.

Lanterns are inseparably associated also in my mind with the lights which they cast over the walls and ceiling of my bedroom when some lantern-bearing sleigh or carriage came up our road at night after I had gone to bed or had been awakened later by the sound of bells or by the clop of horses' feet and the grinding of wagon wheels. These lights were, indeed, among the most vivid and enduring impressions of my childhood. I loved to watch them moving slowly across the ceiling in long bright bars and broken rectangles of yellow radiance, illuminating the darkness of my room. I was glad that our hill was long and steep so that, as the horses made but slow progress, the bars of light moved slowly too, beginning to brighten the black windowpanes, marching up the walls, unsteadily streaming across the white ceiling, moving on and on until they reached the opposite wall and at last flickered away.

I knew that they only came from the lanterns of people driving homeward at night, but they seemed to me especially designed for my delight; and I never ceased to wonder that the ill-smelling tin objects which I had to trim and care for could produce such glory and excitement.

7

A STRANGE DREAM

IN THE early years of my childhood I was assailed by a strange and recurrent dream which filled me with indescribable terror over its nature and with dread over its habit of reappearance. I never told it to anyone, perhaps in fear lest the telling of it would result in its coming again; but I remember that I used to listen to the frequently related dreams of others with envious wonder that they could describe with such apparent eagerness the amusing or ominous details of their own visitations.

The telling of dreams in the late eighteen-nineties, at least in rural communities like our own, was a common contribution not only to family breakfast tables, but to social gatherings of all sorts. In those days the researches of psychologists into the nature both of dreams and of dreamers had not yet resulted in any self-conscious wariness on the part of narrators. Our elders were much given to the rehearsal of dreams and nightmares either to enliven conversation by amusement or terror, as the case might be, or to utter warnings, or to foretell the future. For in common with the ancients, they believed that dreams might well mean omens or prophecies, sometimes pleasant but more often not.

My mother, whose dreams were many and various, was endowed, so everyone believed, with the power of discerning the future by means of them; and I must admit that any number of coincidences, if such they were, supported this belief. If she told us at breakfast that she had dreamed of the presence of some relative or friend among us, nine times out of ten before the day drew to a close that person would actually appear. Once she had a horrible nightmare in which all of us were swimming and some of us drowning in seas of curdled milk; and she narrated this with so much vividness in the morning that none of us was surprised when a few days later the lower band on our churn gave way with dire consequences to the kitchen floor and to our weekly supply of butter. She dreamed also rather frequently that my father was in the White House. We always regretted her eager recounting of this dream since it had the effect of irritating my father, who perhaps felt that he had not realized his full powers and had disappointed her and us by becoming only a country lawyer.

My strange childhood dream possessed, however, no rewarding features of any sort, nor has it taken these upon itself in its recurrences over many years. I think the reason I did not, indeed could not, as a child recount it to anyone lay not so much in the fear of its return as in the recognition that its terrors, though real, were so intangible that they would mean nothing at all if put into words. The dream was, in fact, about nothing. Therein lay and still lies its panic and its dread.

As I look back upon this dream, I realize that I must have been very young when it first assailed me. At least I was still sleeping in a tiny room adjoining that of my parents, a room reserved for the next to the youngest child, the youngest occupying a crib beside their bed. I had, then, graduated from the crib, presumably to make way for my sister Edith, but I had not been moved from the little room. I was, therefore, about three or four years old.

I dreamed that I was alone on some immeasurably vast plain. Besides me, there was no one and nothing. The plain, which was everything and everywhere, seemed to be made of white particles, like crystals, which held neither light nor heat nor cold and which, as I tried to define them to myself upon awaking, seemed to be like rock salt, used to freeze our ice-cream in the summer. Over this limitless white expanse there lay a heavy, drifting mist, also white, which concealed the sky, if there was a sky. There was nothing visible on this endless waste, not a tree, or a rock, or even a hill. It was completely boundless and flat, and I somehow knew that far beyond the reach of my eyes it was the same.

In this dream I walked across this desolate expanse in a strange obscurity, neither dark nor light. And even more terrifying than the dimness, the utter silence, and the vastness was the understanding that I must walk alone forever there, for not only could I make no progress, but there was no end to reach. At every step through the white substance my heavy, tired feet sank deeper within it until I thought that I could not draw them out, that at last my whole body would be out of sight, and that I must finally be lost in nothing at all. At every step, too, I looked back to see the impression of my footprints in the white crystals, but they were never there. Even this sign of me and of my endless journey had disappeared.

I do not remember how often I had this dream as a child, but often enough so that it became my terror by night. It has never entirely left me although in late years it has become less frequent. I have never known it to vary in the least detail from its awful original. There is always the empty, white, endless plain; the silence; the half-light; the weight of my sinking feet; the knowledge that I am abandoned, helpless, alone, and that at last I must become nothing at all.

When I was a child and still in the little room, I used to awake screaming in loneliness and fear. My father, I remember, always brought me a drink of water, and my mother shook up my pillow and tucked me in, once I had been induced to lie down again. "There, there," she always said. "It's all right. It's only a dream."

But it was not all right then, nor has it ever been. And I have never been at all sure that it is only a dream.

8

MY GRANDMOTHER AND HER HARBORS

MY grandmother was known throughout our community as a *remarkable* woman, and I am sure she deserved that comprehensive adjective. When as a child I heard it used, I always thought it referred to her life at sea with my grandfather and to the courage she had displayed in many perils and at least one disaster, for she had been shipwrecked on her honeymoon.[1] She loved to tell us stories of the several voyages which she had taken between the years 1852 and 1861. We always listened entranced,

[1] I have written in *A Goodly Heritage* of the seafaring life of my grandmother, a life not uncommon to many New England coast women of her generation.

for she had extraordinary powers of dramatic narration.

As I grew older, I began to understand that she deserved the adjective not so much because of the adventures which her life had generously bestowed upon her as because of her amazing vitality, mostly physical in nature, which no one, even the least perceptive, could help remarking upon. She was the most alive person I have ever known, simply in terms of breath and being. She was quick, restless, eager, excitable, resilient, impatient, and literally teeming with energy. She was also pretty, vain, charming, loquacious, persuasive, and self-centered. She loved attention, and she never wanted for it.

My father always treated her with the utmost respect, as, indeed, did my mother; and both demanded from us children the same deferential behavior toward her. She always sat opposite my father at the table in the place which, we felt, belonged rightly to my mother; and when my father ushered the long line of us into our pew at church, my grandmother always went in first. Since she grew deaf while she was still at middle age and during her later years was almost totally devoid of hearing, this deference not infrequently exacted no small amount of patience; but any lack of it on our part met with severe reprimand or punishment. She adored my father, her only son, with all the ardor she had left after her lavish expenditure of it elsewhere; yet her devotion, though intense, lacked that tenderness which requires reflection, and for reflection she had neither time nor natural inclination. She held also deep admiration for my mother, or at least admiration, without too much understanding of the adjective.

In spite of her deafness, she was the lively center of every gathering, large or small, and perhaps for that reason she loved every sort of social occasion and rarely missed one. The church, of course, in those days afforded her opportunities for this indulgence; and she was the bulwark, if not of its faith, at least of its more earthly activities. She honestly believed herself a religious woman and was occasionally eloquent, even sententious, concerning this life as but a preparation for the next; but her avidness for the excitements which her particular life yielded her, or could be made to yield, left little time for truly religious practices, which alas! also demanded a measure of quietude and reflection.

Whenever a sad dearth of calls, sewing-bees, and church suppers settled upon us, she fell back upon her own resources for enjoyment and actually made out rather well. She never missed, except in the wildest weather, her daily walk to the village, setting forth briskly and returning some hours later with the same lively step and with all the latest tidings. She loved to range the woods and pastures after spruce tips and wintergreen for her famous spruce beer, which she made several times each year. I imagine that she used to talk to herself on these otherwise solitary excursions, for she was much given to this practice. We often overheard her chatting in her room, apparently making up dialogues in which she doubtless took the leading parts. Whether these were purely fictional or whether she was preparing herself for some emergency in which certain tricks of diction and of manner might be provocative, we never knew, for she never raised her voice sufficiently for us to be sure.

Upon her return from some especially long jaunt into the woods, her black sateen apron laden with her spoils, my mother would suggest a cup of tea and a rest. My grandmother always graciously accepted the tea, but she scorned the idea of a rest.

"But you must be tired," my mother would scream solicitously.

"Why tired?" my grandmother always said. "I'm not tired. I've had a lovely time. Who wants to rest?"

She was always able, also, to extract vicarious excitement from books, for she was an avid reader though a superficial one. Luckily for her Mr. A. Conan Doyle was at the height of his production during her later years and enlivened her days when really monstrous weather kept her indoors, as did Anna Katherine Green, Mr. E. P. Roe, and Marie Corelli. Nor did she ever outgrow her passion for adventure, and loved Jules Verne and R. L. S.

The weather itself held perennial fascination for her, especially since she claimed that she understood its ways, and often violently disputed even the weather vane on the church steeple to its discomfiture and her triumph. She made her forecasts by all manner of devices, the interpretation of which she would never divulge. Sometimes she rubbed Dolly Moses' fur in a dark closet; sometimes she studied pine cones, of which she kept a supply in the woodshed; and from such researches she uttered prophecies which often bore out her alleged powers. Her one apparently unfailing means of prognostication, however, was her habit of lapping the index and middle finger of her right hand and holding these high above her head in the middle of our treeless field until, from some mysterious action of the air upon them, she knew beyond a doubt what sort of weather the morrow must bring forth.

With all her prodigious vitality she was not given to prejudices or even to extreme dislikes. Perhaps her inordinate capacity for pleasure left no room within her mind for harsh judgments. She disliked Aunt Mi intensely, it is true, largely because Aunt Mi, as my grandmother rather acutely said, was *dead on her feet.* And she had a distinct aversion to kittens, with which Dolly Moses liberally supplied us at least twice each year. Here her dislike resulted in helpful action, for she was perfectly willing, if not eager, to drown any number of them in the brook which flowed seaward a short distance behind our house.

I distinctly remember one of these many occasions when, after a return from her annual six months' sojourn with my aunt, her only daughter, she discovered to her disgust that three kittens had been allowed to reach that winning stage of their life which made their extinction impossible for any of us. Even before she had changed her traveling clothes, she procured a meal-bag, into which she dumped all three kittens, amid our tears, and started through the fields toward the brook. Whether she was less thorough in her methods than usual or whether her victims had already savored too happily of existence to relinquish it without a struggle, I do not know; but when a quarter of an hour later she came tripping back home, three drenched kittens slunk behind her through the grass at a safe and respectful distance. She herself thought their survival intensely amusing, gallantly acknowledged herself outwitted, and, once she had dried the kittens, set forth with them in a basket to procure homes for them among her countless friends.

She had a quick and lively imagination, which, I am sure, afforded her equally quick delight, but which rarely, if ever, endured long enough to yield the resources of afterthought, or of meanings and understandings. It was peculiarly associative in quality, and yet it did not, apparently, prolong those pleasures which to the sensitive mind are the immortal gifts of association and relation. Yet, although her imagination was of the fugitive variety, bursting like a shower of rockets into brief, flashing life, its insight was capable of affording enduring riches to others, among whom I was one.

Those things which most intimately concerned her, whether objects or possessions, pastimes or places, fair or furious weather, were constantly associated in her fleeting imagination with her years at sea as a young woman. This association was especially marked in the matter of places, of foreign cities and harbors. She had hated and feared the sea itself, its perils, the discomforts of life aboard ship, and,

I am sure, the endless days of forced inactivity, so that quite naturally ports and harbors meant, first of all, safety, and, in delightful addition, places where she could enjoy unfamiliar sights and sounds and the exciting society which many foreign ports always offered to shipmasters and their wives. These pleasures she would recount over and over: a serenade accorded her in Cadiz, which was one of my grandfather's frequent ports of call; a royal procession in London and her sight of Queen Victoria, then young like herself; gay parties in Rio, or Canton, or Singapore. She would describe, too, what it was like to see blue, distant land after interminable days of water, to slip into some harbor, to see houses, trees, people, to know that fresh food awaited one, and space to move about in, and things to do.

These harbors with their offerings of security and amusement never, I am sure, left her mind, and probably for that reason their familiar outlines were recreated for her in the sky as she scanned it for signs of weather. I was around ten or eleven when her imagination transferred to my own the fancy that the clouds, especially at sunset, framed harbors with headlands and reefs, islands, inlets, channels, and distant mountains. She would designate the harbors, pointing them out excitedly to us children, her index finger following each curve and line. Rio, with its heights above the sea; San Francisco, a wide golden space of sky with mountain ranges behind it and islands in the foreground; Riga, cold and desolate in the winter with its gray shores of cloud. Once she had identified them to her own satisfaction, she returned at once to the things which had happened to her here and there.

Even had I known any specific harbor except our own quiet one, I do not think I should have searched for its counterpart in the sky. It was the discovery that one at will could translate clouds into harbors which excited me as a child. It was quite enough for me, then as now, to see them lying low and still at sunset, with their bays and encircling shore lines, their hills and islands, sharp and clear in the fading light, and, like my grandmother's remembered harbors, offering security and pleasure, if of another sort.

My grandmother died unwillingly at eighty-seven and, happily, very quickly, with not so much as a minute for reflection.

9

TWO DAYS OF DISCOVERY

THE NORMAL life of a child before the turbulent years of adolescence is mostly a succession of similar days, brightened now and again by unusual events and pastimes or darkened by the embarrassment of punishments or by small, easily assuaged sorrows. These early days and months with their familiar happenings and attendant natural emotions would seem to determine the character of our later years, of our thoughts and attitudes, simply by means of their constant repetition; yet in point of fact they in the mass or as figures on a dial determine very little. This truth is borne out again and again by the vague memories which most of us possess concerning our years between the ages of five and thirteen. As we look back upon those years, they tend to merge one into another, to become in memory a succession of inseparable days of which few, if any, stand out sharply *as* days even in the most sensitive and imaginative minds. Birthdays, certain Christmases, and special holidays are sometimes an exception because of some extraordinary excitement connected therewith, although even with these red-letter days the quality, the reality usually has been lost somewhere in their mere outward trappings. For the most part, to a child a day is merely a day, one indistinguishable from another in their countless number.

For this reason I have always cherished a sense of grateful surprise over the clear recollection of two days in my own childhood, which stand out as points in time because of their peculiar quality, intangible though very real. Perhaps, indeed, these days are not so much remembered as unconsciously salvaged, rescued from the oblivion of numberless other days to claim a place in my mind as permanent possessions. Little actually happened upon either of them, and yet they remain in my imagination like shafts of bright sunlight illuminating the dark corridors of time. One was a winter day when I was perhaps eleven years old; the other a day in spring when I was about the same age. The circumstances attendant on these days, why I was where I was, have quite faded from my memory. I recall only the strange and heretofore unapprehended meanings of the days themselves to my little life.

THE WHITE GATE

I

The day in winter was one of bitter cold, cold which, I think, must have suddenly smitten our isolated region of the Maine coast in the afternoon, else I should not have been allowed out by myself. Apparently I had gone, as we children occasionally did, in the morning to spend the day with playmates who lived two or three miles away on some outlying farm; for in my childhood to trudge two or three or even five miles through the countryside was not unusual, provided our parents were clearly aware of our *terminus ad quem* and approved of it. *To spend the day*, a phrase now seldom used since the increased tempo of life has made such leisurely occupation seemingly impossible, was always an adventure to us; and I have no doubt that I had set forth on my long walk that morning with keen excitement even though I now recall nothing of it or of my destination. What I do remember with extreme clarity is my return home in the afternoon along the snowy country road, much of which ran through deep woods on either side.

Probably both pain and fear contributed to the tenacious hold which this particular day has throughout the years kept upon my memory; and yet neither of them can be held responsible for the discovery which it afforded me. Indeed, the discovery, frail in itself, would hardly seem able to combat such suffering as I endured on that long walk home. I shall never forget how cold I was, or how the bitter air above and around me seemed an enemy bent on my destruction. The sky, I remember, was clear and cloudless and of a pale blue. There was no wind. As I trudged onward and the sun behind me sank lower, the blue of the sky faded to silver, shining like ice. My chest hurt me as I breathed the piercing air; my feet in my high overshoes were heavy and numb, yet ached cruelly with every step. I tried to run, but the pain of the cold in my lungs and feet made running impossible. I was afraid, and began to cry until I realized with terror that my tears were freezing on my cheeks. Never, except in my strange dream, had I felt so abandoned and alone. I looked behind me in the hope of some sleigh or sledge which would take me home; but there was no sight of anything warm or human, no sound of friendly bells. I was alone on what seemed an interminable road, surrounded by dark trees in deep snow, and the cold sun was almost out of sight.

I was descending a hill, my heavy feet slipping in its snowy ruts, when I made my discovery. I had taken off my red mittens here and held them between my teeth while I tried to ease the pain in my fingers by pushing my hands inside my coat and into the warm hollows beneath my shoulders. But this only exposed my chest to the cold, and I hastily again drew on my mittens, now colder themselves, and began to thrash my arms against my sides. My tears felt hot behind my eyes, but I did not dare to cry.

At the foot of the hill an icebound stream crossed the road beneath a wooden bridge, and along its course the woods had given way on either side to a small clearing. I knew the place well, for we children often came here in the summer in search of the brilliant cardinal flowers which blossomed among the thick grasses farther up the brook. I do not know why I stopped on the wooden bridge, as I must have wanted only to reach home where there would be warmth and familiar life. I had more than a mile to travel, and the sun had already gone. But I did stop. I leaned against the wooden railing of the bridge and looked up the clearing along the course of the brook. I remember that with all my weariness and my acute suffering from the cold I wondered why the black water still swirled beneath the pale blue ice, forming bubbles here and there and tiny whirlpools, and sounding clear notes in the surrounding silence.

Then I suddenly saw that the soft white snow on either side of the stream was cut and marked by the tracks of some creatures who had not long before scurried across it on their way to the woods. The identity of the creatures did not come to my mind, whether they were rabbits, or squirrels, or what not. It was their tiny footprints on the snow which held me and made me forget the bitter cold. The footprints were frail and beautiful, delicate marks in a pattern of threes. They lay within the otherwise unbroken whiteness, separated, each distinct and perfect. They followed the brook for several feet on either side, then curved away at almost the same point in a wavering arc toward the dark spruces. I must have seen them a hundred times; yet I had never seen them before. They became for me in those moments a living experience, the entire content of a day, its reality, its only meaning.

I did not, of course, interpret them in such terms or even in ideas. They were simply there as they had never been before. They were new and strange, and although their sudden appeal was inexpressible and intangible, it was mysterious and real. I remember that the snow turned from white to pale blue as I stood there in the bitter cold and that the tiny footmarks in the gathering darkness were becoming black and indistinct. I did not know then why I hated to leave them, or why, as I pushed my numb and heavy feet along the road, I had forgotten the ache in them and in my fingers and had lost my loneliness and fear.

When a little farther on I heard the sound of sleighbells and saw my father in our yellow pung anxiously driving to fetch me, I was half regretful. Only a few minutes before, he would have meant warmth and safety, but now he seemed an intruder upon my thrilling secret.

II

More intangible and yet equally real in its effect was that other day in my childhood which I have never forgotten. Its special quality was not impressed upon me by physical pain or by fear, nor did it grant me through so clear an outward and visible sign its inward and spiritual grace. I have often, indeed, wondered why it has lingered in my mind through all these many years; but there it is, distinct, luminous, and inviolable.

It was a day in spring, and it must have been in early spring, for we had not as yet been allowed to cast off our winter underwear, and as the warmth of the morning increased, it felt cumbrous and uncomfortable. I have no remembrance of where I had been when the peculiar and essential meaning of the day stole over me, but probably on some errand to the village. I know that I was coming up the board sidewalk which led past the picket fence surrounding our orchard when all at once I felt an odd quickening within me.

There had been a white mist in the early morning from a heavy rainfall during the night, and the sun was just then breaking through it in long rays of light. I felt suddenly surrounded by light and half frightened by the equally sudden perception of it. I walked slowly up the sidewalk until I reached the white gate, where I stopped, for I was puzzled and bewildered.

Light to me before this had been the absence of darkness, the assurance of safety, of the ordinary and the familiar; and I could not understand why these rays of light dispelling the mist, this unexpected, sudden effulgence, seemed so different from daylight in its usual sense. I felt as though something were happening inside me, for I seemed all at once incomprehensibly alive and new, even as if I had just been born.

I did not open the gate and enter the driveway, for my home was at that moment unfamiliar, intrusive, unwelcome, and singularly far removed from me. I stood instead with my back against the gate. I had the curious thought that I was waiting for something to happen, for something to be explained to me, although I had no notion of what that something was. There was no one coming or going along the muddy road. I was alone with my mystery, which disturbed and troubled me.

Then I saw how the sunlight was irradiating everything, how the weather vane on the church steeple gleamed with it, how the brown puddles in the road glistened, how the sodden grasses in the field opposite sparkled from millions of shining drops. I became aware of the sound of water everywhere, dripping from the bare branches of the orchard trees, running through the grassy ditch on either side of the gate, falling from the eaves of the house into the pools below with round musical notes. In the stillness of the air I could hear the freed, full water of the brook beyond our field, falling over the dam and rushing through the mill-race. All my small world was transfigured by light, motion, and sound; and I in my worn old reefer and stocking-cap seemed to be in some odd way transfigured also.

I do not know how long I stood outside the gate, watching and listening, waiting for something strange and overwhelming to become clear; for I felt as though I myself were filled with light and motion, as though I had never before been truly awake. I was suddenly afraid of the familiar, commonplace things in the house and of my family, who must, I thought, see at once that I was somehow different and ask to my embarrassment whatever had happened to me.

Needless to say, no one in the household was in the least aware of my transfiguration. To them I was as ordinary and usual as I had always been. Yet the meaning of the day never entirely left me, becoming like the frail tracks in the unbroken snow a secret—guarded, inexplainable, but forever real.

10

PIGEONS

OF ALL the many largesses now granted me by summer and early autumn on an isolated point of land on the Maine coast, none is more satisfying than the migrations of birds in late September and early October. I do not mean so much the leisurely passing southward of birds singly or in pairs, the shy appearance for a few days of thrushes or of warblers who alight in my spruces for rest or scratch about among the blueberry bushes for food against another stage of their long flights. These also afford pleasure, as do the perfect formations of wild geese flying high over the sea, bearing always south beyond the islands and headlands. Neither, however, offers the excitement of those vast mass migrations which sweep overhead usually just at dawn.

I first became aware of them several years ago when I was awakened one morning in the earliest light by a heavy whirr of wings and by plaintive calls somewhere outside my open window and seemingly not far above my house. The next morning I rose in the dark and went out-of-doors, hardly daring to hope that this miracle could take place on two consecutive days. My faint hope, however, was generously fulfilled.

After I had stood for a few minutes in the half-light, looking seaward where our rocky point juts into the open Atlantic, I became conscious, as the eastern sky brightened, of a dark, serrated cloud moving in from the water and coming steadily on over the land. As it drew nearer, I heard the rush of wings, faint at first like the quivering of small leaves in a light wind. Then, for fully five minutes and only some thirty feet above my head, a vast multitude of birds flew through the air, on and on in countless thousands, birds impossible to distinguish one from another even had the light been stronger. Occasionally some called in short, sharp notes, but for the most part they flew silently, the whirr of their wings now increasing to a hum like the sound of bees. They passed in so close a mass that it was impossible to see the motions of their flight until, as they swept out of sight and became but a blur in the distant sky, a few hundred stragglers, perhaps finding the speed too swift, revealed themselves more clearly as small birds, warblers, perhaps, or sparrows, flying on and on with a constant restless fluttering. For they could not rest upon the air as gulls rest and soar, but had to keep always in agitated motion, beating the atmosphere with frail, outstretched wings.

The teasing thoughts of their gathering by thousands in some unknown place, their flight over vast reaches of sea from whence they had obviously come, their sure knowledge of their far destination, their frailty against winds and rain, have excited my mind ever since I first watched their passage. Always, as I see them year by year, I wonder what it is precisely which makes a flight of birds so poignant a manifestation of the mystery of creation; and I realize as I wonder that my initial sense of this mystery was born long ago in my childhood when we allowed pigeons to live in the loft of our barn.

My father often questioned, and most audibly, why he put up with our pigeons when he might easily have closed the two tiny windows of their dovecote and compelled them to go elsewhere. They were clearly only a nuisance, he said. They had dirty habits which necessitated the cleaning of their quarters several times a season, an unpleasant job which he would not do himself and which, therefore, meant the paying out of good money to someone who would. They were quite unfeeling birds with cold yellow eyes and with apparently no affection for us and no gratitude for their home, which was under the topmost eaves of our barn. We never fed them, for this would have encouraged their alighting in the driveway and messing up its gravel with their droppings and their feathers. They seemed, indeed, entirely separated from us; but they were not separated, simply because of their sweeping flights from their cote to some unknown place in the morning and the whirr of their wings as they returned home at the close of the day.

I cannot remember when I was unaware of this whirr of wings or of the contented, subdued, drowsy murmuring when they had come back to their dovecote. Both seem a part of my earliest childhood, perhaps the first sounds outside our house of which I was fully conscious. We children missed the pigeons when they left us in the autumn for some unknown winter haven and eagerly awaited their return, not because we loved them in the least, but because they brought excitement and beauty to our lives.

There were not many of them in our flock, perhaps twenty or thirty, and they were all either blue or white. The blue had shining throats of many colors; and the white were of an almost unimaginable whiteness. My father insisted that they were the selfsame ones year by year, commenting with scorn that there must be yet another family somewhere as foolish and stupid as we were, with another barn which harbored them. To prove his irritable contention he seized a dozen of them one summer evening while the rest of the flock squawked and fluttered around his head and banded their legs with tiny bits of tin. He was right. The next year the banded ones were back in our dovecote.

I suppose our pigeons must have laid eggs and hatched

their young, but I have no recollection of such activity. All their more personal traits were seemingly of little interest to us. We cherished no anxiety for them as we did for the robins who nested each year in the woodbine over the back porch, laid four blue eggs, and reared their awkward fledglings. We associated our pigeons with nothing but their sound and their flight; yet these in themselves were no small compensations.

When they left their dovecote in the morning in one flock, they flew westward past the church and out of sight beyond the distant trees. They always set forth with a great stir of wings, coming one by one from their little windows and fluttering about in the air outside until all were ready. They flew low at first and fairly far apart over our driveway until they reached the field across the road, where they formed a more compact flock and rose high into the air. Where they went we never knew, or how they spent their days. But we always awaited their return home with that expectancy which returns always, for some odd reason, excite in greater measure than departures.

The pigeons were invariably punctual, but their coming home seemed to be governed solely by the light and to have no connection with mere time. I am sure they returned at the same instant on rainy or cloudy days; but I remember their homeward flight past the church, over the field, and toward our gate only on clear afternoons and evenings when our orchard was flooded with the last rays of the sun. When they reached the field, they again broke their close formation, dropped low in the air, and flew just above our heads with a whirr of wings toward the barn. The sun caught their feathers, blue and iridescent and white, and cast moving shadows of their outstretched wings upon the white gravel of the driveway and upon the orchard grass. And as they fluttered about in the bright air outside their windows, waiting their turns to enter their dovecote, their restless stirrings caused other shadows to move across the white clapboards of our barn.

We never felt we were quite complete as a family until our untidy, thankless pigeons had winged their way home for the night.

11

THE BIRTH OF AN ISLAND

WHENEVER I return, as I frequently do, to the village where I was born and reared and to our old house still owned and occupied by members of my family, I never fail to cross the fields to the brook to see the island there, which at the age of ten I saw born in the running water. It is a large island now after more than fifty years of growth, so large, indeed, that one can easily cross the brook upon it by only a fairly long step from one rocky bank to the other. Fair-sized trees grow on it now, grass and reeds, and, I am told, violets blossom there in the spring, both purple and white.

When I was ten, there was no island at all. The brook then hurried on over its bed of ledges and coarse gravel toward the milldam only fifty feet away where it widened into a deep, dark pool, the highest of its waters falling in pale brown sheets, smooth and shining, over the dam to turn the great wheel of the sawmill which stood below it. The dam is still there, but it has become sodden and grass-grown, and little water flows over it now, for the island has retarded the course of the brook, and the pool is far less wide and deep than it used to be when I was young. Nor is there longer any use for a millwheel turned by water.

This island, now some twenty feet long and nearly as wide, has always held a special place in my imagination since I saw it born and watched it with anxiety through several years of my childhood lest the spring freshets should dislodge its insecure beginnings and end its life by sweeping them over the dam. I distinctly remember the morning of its birth. It was May Day, and I had been wading up the brook after the fragile white blossoms of the shadbush, or sugar pear, as we called it then; for we were that evening to hang our homemade May baskets, filled with flowers, on the front doors of our playmates and neighbors. It was an unusual May Day, I had thought gratefully, as I paddled my way around the slippery rocks and through the cold waters, for it was seldom that the wild cherry and sugar pear were in blossom or even in full bud in time for the hanging of May baskets.

When I came down again and stopped on our favorite

sloping ledge to put on my stockings and shoes, I saw in the middle of the stream a small drifting mass of knotted grasses, held together by a branch of the same sugar pear which I had been gathering for my cornucopias. The white flowers in the brown water held my attention; and as I watched them carried downstream, I saw them suddenly stopped by two jutting rocks and held between them. The water ran by on either side, high from the spring rains and from earlier melting snow and ice; yet the sugar pear and the grasses remained wedged between the rocks. Having recently read about the formation of deltas in my geography book, for I had just begun that study and felt vastly proud of my new learning, I watched with keen excitement, and in the course of half an hour saw other floating bits of twigs and chips increase the size of the tiny island, which I at once appropriated as my own, I having been the sole witness of its birth.

I could not believe that so small a cluster of twigs and grasses could possibly withstand the onrush of the water; yet I fervently hoped that it might. I went almost daily to the brook throughout all that spring and summer, gaining renewed hope and confidence with every inspection of my island, which I named Sugar Pear Island after its parentage. The early autumn found Sugar Pear still an island; and I was entranced to see that some red leaves of the swamp maple, drifting down the stream, had halted there to add bright color to its dun and still swaying surface. One late September day, worried by its motion, I waded out to test for myself its staying qualities and found to my intense delight that there was sand beneath it and that some of its watery ingredients seemed well rooted therein. I realized as I stood there (wet to the waist and soberly counting the cost of my research once I had reached home) that I could myself uproot my island with only a few stout tugs of my hands. Some Sundays afterward when I heard in church that God *taketh up the isles as a very little thing*, I felt an odd kinship with Him, at least in relation to Sugar Pear.

All through the winter when the brook was frozen except in its deepest channels, I kept thinking of my island, now tightly bound in ice, and saw as I walked from time to time over the bridge above the millpond how its two protecting rocks were now two mounds of snow. The test of its endurance would come, I knew, with the freshets and floods of another spring, and again I waited with anxiety to know its fate. Its mounds of snow melted in April; and there it was, no longer swaying with the motion of the water, but securely anchored in the sand.

Sugar Pear grew slowly, yet I had no fears for it after its first precarious year of life. Every spring more drifting grasses, leaves, and twigs enlarged its boundaries and, I felt sure, more grains of sand increased its firm foundation. In times of flood, to be sure, when the waters of the brook *roared and were troubled*, it was covered *with the deep as with a garment*, but it always emerged when the waters, like those of Noah, *were abated*. After three or four years it sprouted some reedy grass of its own; and by that time the two jutting rocks, once its protectors, indeed its very means of existence, formed its moss-grown center. It was still a tiny island when I had entered my teens, but it was large enough on its fifth anniversary to grow a small blue iris among spiked green leaves. And when I went away to school at seventeen, my brother Edward had claimed its two mossy rocks as a good place to stand with his alder pole and tin can of worms while he fished for trout in the rippling water which flowed by on either side.

He and my sisters with our playmates began, of course, to notice it after it had weathered a year or so of life and loved also to watch it grow spring by spring. It was always the *new island* to them, but it was *Sugar Pear Island* to me. I never told its name to anyone or explained my proprietorship; but the secret affinity I felt for it as a child has lasted throughout my life. Two years ago in the spring when I was in our village and took my usual walk to the brook to see how it was faring, I saw among its chokecherries and alders a flowering bush of sugar pear. I felt immeasurably gratified to realize that it had justified my christening of it on a May Day many years ago.

12

THE DOCTOR'S SAUCER

AMONG the dishes in our china cupboard when I was a child was a glass saucedish which, since it was the only one of its kind and too small for pickles or preserves in a family so large as ours, was seldom used at meals. We were very fond of it, however, since it was of an enticing shape, round and deep, and had encircling its rim a line of tiny stars cut into the glass. Perhaps because of its importance to us, it was early set apart by my mother as *the doctor's saucer*, although in reality it was not a saucer at all, or even strictly a saucedish, but, rather, a little glass bowl. I always see it holding some flat pink pills, shaped like small lozenges, which the doctor invariably left upon those rare and momentous occasions when he called professionally upon us. I do not think I ever wondered what healing properties these pills contained or why they were always the same in size and color whatever the nature of the illness. The saucedish with its awesome contents was, instead, a symbol to me of that intense excitement which literally galvanized our entire household before, during, and immediately after the doctor's visit.

The one occasion when the doctor came as a matter of course, without preliminary and anxious discussion on the part of our parents as to the wisdom of summoning outside counsel to our aid, was the arrival of a new baby. Since this event, however, was always marked by our absence, we older children being given over to the care of relatives or friends for the necessary time involved, we were not aware of what went on at home. We were simply taken under some hospitable rooftree for a day or a night and, after all was safely over, brought back home to see our new brother or sister. I do not remember that the *whys* or the *wherefores* of this new member of our family troubled us overmuch, nor do I recall any explanatory falsehoods which doubtless were told us, although I myself comfortably thought that the doctor somehow kept babies somewhere and brought them wherever they were wanted. Our baby was simply with us to claim most of our mother's attention and care and not a little of our own; and we adjusted to the new situation without too much concern on anyone's part.

Cash outlay for new life was never questioned, since it was inevitable. My father paid the doctor, as I learned long afterward, five dollars for each of us, which, with two follow-up visits to my mother and the baby at one dollar and a half each, made the purely monetary cost of my sisters, my brother, and me eight dollars per child. Our second lot of four children may have commanded a slightly higher price, but I doubt if it rose excessively, at least in our locality, even with the beginning of a new century. To the original eight dollars were added the two weeks' services of some village or country woman, who acted as midwife and nurse and who was paid two dollars a week. Still, even with this extra expense, I reckon that the total initial cost of each of us, with an allowance for necessary sundries, could not have exceeded fifteen dollars. And I have always taken pleasure in the realization that whatever financial expenditures, not to mention other anxieties, I may later have cost my parents, at least my actual advent into this world was not too great a drain upon their modest cash resources in the year 1887.

To *summon* the doctor in the ordinary course of human events was, however, quite another matter, so infrequent and so startling that his saucer with its pink pills has remained in my imagination as a sacred symbol not only of the solemn upheaval of our household, but of our importance as a family. Such calls were never decided upon lightly in any country family at the turn of the century; and ours was no exception to the rule. They meant not only expense, but the reluctant admission of mothers that they were not competent to deal single-handed with the illness in question. They meant also an anxious flurry of the entire community; for the news that any family *had had the doctor* was bound to travel rapidly and widely, to cause general alarm and concern, and to be commonly interpreted not as a precautionary measure, but as a last resort.

My mother's talents in dealing with illness were exceptional even in a day when most mothers of large families were supposed to be well versed in the diagnosis of common disorders and in the knowledge of country remedies. She could gauge a fever; identify most rashes; treat burns, cuts, bruises, sprains, and boils; tie up a sore throat in a stocking still warm from a child's foot; cure earache by the insertion in the ear of a hot raisin; make poultices of bread and milk and plasters of lard and mustard or of skunks' grease. She knew all about the stealthy approach of croup and daily attended our creosote lamp so that it might not fail during possible nightly ravages. She was familiar with all ailments of the stomach, whether cholera morbus, summer complaint, or simple colic, and would cheerfully decide whether hot ginger tea, essence of peppermint, or an emetic was the wisest means of cure. She kept on the top shelf of a small wall cupboard in her bedroom a square black case of homeopathic remedies, little glass phials of tiny white pills labeled *aconite*, *belladonna*, *nux vomica*, and other less familiar names; and when any one of us seemed feverish or "out of sorts" in any other way, she would administer a few of these pills at nightfall and wait in quiet confidence for the morrow. Therefore, whenever an indisposition lingered overlong and we heard her say to my father, "If that child is not really better in the morning, I think we must seriously consider calling in the doctor," we knew that matters were grave, indeed. On such rare nights I went to bed not only tense from excitement, but, I am afraid, besieged by the guilty hope that the morning would bring added consternation instead of relief. Even the stricken, in all his or her discomfort, was not entirely proof against such dreams and desires, for to be able to relate at school that one had been so ill as to be under the doctor's care for even a single visit denoted signal achievement and triumph.

We had two doctors in our village when I was a child, though the existence of even one would have been a serious problem had not the yearly supply of babies solved it in some measure. The one whom we employed, not only to bring us a baby but whenever more usual matters came to a crisis, lived next door to us. He was a tall, rather quiet man, who had a passion for local history and plenty of time to indulge it. He loved to potter around his vegetable garden and to saw and split wood, a generous supply of which he kept in his yard. One of the front rooms of his large white house served as his office, a rather untidy room cluttered by stuffed birds, books, and papers. Here he received patients who were able to consult him at home and saved fifty cents or a dollar by so doing since his own visits afield were priced from one to two dollars each, depending on the distance.

He had a genius for profanity of the quiet, even reverent sort and sprinkled his unprofessional conversation rather generously with it. This habit amused my father, disturbed my mother, and struck added awe into us children. Perhaps the doctor's profanity was helpful in tempering my father's irritation toward his politics. For he was not merely himself a staunch Democrat, but also the acknowledged leader of the few of that misguided persuasion among us; and only my father's deep respect for him as a physician could possibly have offset this unfortunate and even incredible fact.

When the decision to call the doctor had been irrevocably made and the hour of his approach drew nigh, a vast and awful solemnity descended upon our household. We children who were well except for extreme tension watched from the dining-room windows, all of us washed, combed, and in clean raiment. The patient, if it was summer, was lying in our four-poster in the spare room upstairs, clean, expectant, and important; if it was winter, he or she was in our small downstairs bedroom or on a cot in the living-room beyond the library. In either case the bed was immaculate with fresh linen, and my mother, for once hovering about nervously, was immaculate also in a starched white apron. No one spoke. The slow, heavy ticking of the dining-room clock was the only sound. All eyes were on the doctor's house awaiting the moment when he should emerge therefrom with my father, who had gone to fetch him, walk up the sidewalk, and turn in through our white gate. On our dining-room table, arranged in ceremonial order, were a large white napkin, a pitcher of water with a tumbler beside it, a silver spoon, *and* the doctor's glass saucer. The kitchen was ready also, the kettle boiling on the stove, the sink clean, fresh towels on its shelf together with a flowered washbowl from one of our bedroom sets.

When the doctor preceded my father into our hallway between kitchen and dining-room, he paid little attention to us children though, at a respectful distance, our eyes were riveted upon him. Once he had given his hat into the hands of my father or of Annie, either of whom received it in the manner of an acolyte receiving a biretta from an officiating priest, and greeted my mother with appropriate gravity, he stood for a few minutes, whatever the season, holding his hands over the hot kitchen stove, preparatory, we assumed, to examining his patient. I do not recall that he washed them before his entrance into the sickroom even although all had been made ready for him at the kitchen sink. Then he followed my parents into the library for a preconsultation behind a door closed to us, who still stood hushed and silent in the dining-room and who remained in that unusual state until his return. What went on by the bedside was withheld from us, nor do I think we were much interested in it. It was the extraordinary presence of the doctor within our midst which rendered us inarticulate and entranced, together with the overwhelming sense that we were all concerned in this sudden rupture of our familiar pattern of existence.

When, after another muted conversation in the library,

the doctor returned to the dining-room, followed by my mother and father, he became more aware of our presence, even to the extent of depressing our tongues with the silver spoon and looking at the throat of each of us. "Just in case," he said to my mother. Then he winked at my father and said, "Four birds with one stone." I was used to this familiar expression, with varying numerals, and thought it but a mild pleasantry, until my sister Mildred explained its meaning: that the doctor's inspection of the rest of us would cost my father nothing at all.

At last the climaxing moment came. The doctor opened his big black satchel on the dining-room table, spreading its two parts flat, and, after a few moments' deliberation, chose from its glass bottles the medicines he had decided upon. While he did this, he gave my mother explicit directions for their use which she wrote down carefully with a pencil on a pad of paper. I always waited anxiously for the pink pills, fearing lest among the tiny packets of powders or the red or brown or green liquids, which he poured into little bottles from larger ones, they might be overlooked; but I do not remember that they ever were. He kept a rather large paste-board box of them under a strap in the middle of one side of his satchel; and the moment when he drew out this box and allowed a dozen or more of them to fall into the glass saucedish was to me the crowning point of his visit and the crest of our distinction as a family.

We remained subdued in voice and manner for quite some time after the doctor had gone through our gate and on toward his own house. We could not descend easily or quickly into our everyday ways. We were not too interested, I fear, in the fate of the patient, who during that hour had seemed but a means to an end, the comparatively unexciting cause of a stupendous effect. I remember that I secretly hoped to be sent upon some errand to the village so that I might answer seriously all the many questions which would be asked me, repeating solemnly my mother's remark to us that *all was as well as it could be under the circumstances.* Such errands did sometimes materialize and always were extremely welcome to the ones selected for their performance. But if they did not, there were always the concrete evidences of the doctor's visit on the white mantelpiece in our dining-room. My mother always placed them there, the glass saucedish conspicuously in the center.

On succeeding days, when I saw the doctor setting forth in his top-buggy or sleigh on some call into the country, I wondered enviously if the excited family there had a glass saucedish, consecrated like our own to the pink pills, which, I felt sure, he would leave with them also.

13

HIGH PASTURES

WHENEVER I drive along the coast of Maine from the Piscataqua river to the St. Croix, as I do several times in every summer, I am sadly impressed by the absence of pastures as I knew them when I was a child. Many pastures are still there, of course, in outline at least, although their old log fences have mostly given place to barbed wire; but their original characteristic features, their rocky ledges and boulders, their bare, closely cropped open spaces, their stands of spruces and firs, their clumps of blueberry and huckleberry bushes, have suffered many changes. Their ledges and boulders are now hidden by alders; few neighborhood cows now keep their open spaces open; and their pointed firs and spruces are surrounded and entangled by undergrowth of every sort. Most Maine cows now feed in herds in fields and meadows instead of subsisting on the sparse grass of rocky soil; and, since the vast majority of people even in outlying districts now burn oil instead of wood in their cookstoves, there is no need to clear away the smaller trees as there used to be. Pastures are now disheveled pieces of land, their former nature indistinct or even completely lost.

As I recall the Maine pastures which I knew many years ago, I am inclined to think that they symbolize, or at least represent, certain more or less definite stages in the process of my *becoming*, which Pater calls the process of brain-building in the life of a child. And if in mine, surely in that of countless other country children of my time and place who knew and loved pastures as I did. There were several of the old kind of pastures near my home and to range about in them was an integral part of my childhood. They were all on high land above the sea since the lower land was cut into meadows and fields. One entered each of them through pasture *bars*, framed of three or four well-weathered logs. These were supported by two perpendicular logs, which either were cut with holes into which the horizontal logs slid, or held crosspieces of wood upon which they rested. Small children crawled through the bars; larger ones let one or two down and then replaced them carefully against straying cows; the most adventuresome among us, whether boys or girls, climbed them or even vaulted over them into the pasture.

The features of these familiar pastures were very much the same. Each was high and, therefore, hilly; each had a grove or two of spruces, pines, and firs, with a few clumps of white birches here and there and some thickets of alders, which were in far better control than alders are today since our cows enjoyed their young shoots in the spring; each grew blueberry bushes of the low variety, which afforded berries in late July and August and which in September made a carpet of scarlet, crimson, and purple over much of the pasture; each possessed numberless gray rocks and boulders and, commonly, some ledges as well. And in every pasture there was a small brook flowing over mossy rocks and bordered by ferns.

Our pastures were named usually for their owners. In our neighborhood there were the Hinckley pasture, Dr. Grindle's pasture, the Peters pasture, and the Mountain Pastures; and all of these were occupied from May until October by the cows of the community. Since most families kept a cow but few possessed a pasture, a modest rental was charged each summer by the owner for grazing privileges. Most of the cows wore bells of iron or copper, and we children learned to identify the differing sounds of these bells as we went to fetch our respective animals in the late afternoon and to lead or drive them home.

The Hinckley pasture was the nearest to us, only two small fields away, and it was here that I first began to be aware of the blessings afforded by pastures to children. In the Hinckley pasture was a huge ledge of rock cut into fissures and set about by large boulders. While we were still very young, we were permitted to come here to play *house* on the ledge. We each chose our particular residence, establishing its boundaries carefully by small stones, and proceeded to furnish it by whatever the pasture afforded and by the few bits of broken crockery and odds and ends of cloth which we had been allowed to bring from home. We spent hours on this ledge, sometimes by ourselves, sometimes with enough playmates to make the game of *families* possible. I can still remember when the murmuring of the wind in some pines surrounding the ledges suddenly seemed to me the most comforting of sounds, and how one day I cried bitterly over breaking a cluster of tiny acorn cups which I had found and wanted to keep among my treasures because I saw that it was frail and lovely.

Dr. Grindle's pasture was in reality two pastures, each of considerable size; and since it was farther away and could not afford us a sight of the village houses and the smoke from their chimneys as could the Hinckley, we were not allowed its freedom until we were well on into school age. We loved and yet feared Dr. Grindle's pasture since it possessed wilder features than did the Hinckley. It was a very still pasture, not only owing to its distance from houses, but because of its large groves of tall dark trees which the sun rarely penetrated. One never went there alone; but for groups of three or four it was a wonderful place. After we had let down the bars at the entrance and followed a rocky path to a swamp where red and white trilliums grew, we passed through a dark grove to the second pasture, beyond other bars. The silence of this upper pasture was lonely, even ominous, for the trees grew even thicker and there were no familiar cows, since they preferred the open spaces and the more abundant grass of the lower. Under one group of tall spruces lay the white skeleton of a long-dead horse, a mysterious and frightening object to us. Still, when this had been hurriedly skirted, a slippery path carpeted with pine needles led downward to a really large brook, the upper reaches, indeed, of the brook which moved the mill wheel and in which Sugar Pear Island was born. The sun fell always clear and hot on the brown water of this brook; and once we were there, we forgot the fearsome aspects of the dark trees and the sinister white bones under them. I used to wish around the age of nine that I had sufficient courage to come to this brook alone, for its riches were immeasurable.

Chief among these were dragonflies in great number. They were commonly called *devils' darning needles*, but I did not like the name since to me they suggested nothing so ordinary as a darning needle. I loved to perch on a high rock above a shallow pool with a bottom of yellow sand and watch the brilliant blue of their long, thin bodies change to green, gold, and purple in the sun. Their wings were transparent lines of light as they darted across the water of the pool, skimming and circling like miniature swallows. Sometimes one would settle on a reed, or a lily pad, or the frond of a fern, fold its shining wings close to its sides, and rest there like a tiny jeweled arrow; sometimes, even while it rested, it would spread its wings, revealing them as cut into hundreds of little windowpanes, so small and perfect as to be unbelievable. For the most part, however, the dragonflies skimmed constantly over the water, making a thin whirr or whine in the air. When the light was especially clear in late morning or early afternoon, they cast quick shadows upon the pool, which seemed to quiver with their colors against the yellow sand. They never appeared to be about any business of their own like bees, or water spiders, or butterflies; but only to dart and sparkle above the brook for the joy of doing so. This thought, at first only a fancy as I watched them summer by summer, became one day saddened by truth. For I took one from the reed on which it hung in order to look at it more closely. Then, with a feeling almost akin to terror, I felt its body, so recently a sharp flame in the sunlight, become inert and sluggish and saw that its brilliant colors were fading within the warm, moist prison of my hand.

The Peters pasture, which I knew almost too well during my twelfth summer, held, I am sure, the same treasures as did the others, but I remember it for vastly different reasons. It lay half a mile from our house, beyond the village, beyond the graveyard on its hill, and above a small cove of the bay. Our cow, Constancy, was pastured within it during that summer, and it was my job to drive her there in the morning and to go to fetch her at night.

Constancy was a mild cow as cows go, but she either possessed no sense of time or an aversion to time itself, for she was almost never at the pasture bars when toward suppertime I arrived there to get her. She loved to hide away in swamps and alder thickets; and during that summer she was left completely to her own devices since she was the only cow there and hence was uninfluenced by less individualistic companions. This fact meant that I also was companionless not only when I drove her to and fro but when I was obliged to find her wherever she might be.

The summer of my twelfth year was marked for me by new and strange emotions which smote me at unpredictable times with no apparent reason. I was given to bursting into storms of tears, to feeling unhappy and forsaken, and to finding myself frightened by things which heretofore had held no fears whatsoever. I was often irritable at home, and, although I doubtless deserved all the parental reproofs which I generously received, they seemed to me unfair and often resulted in a sense of alienation and loneliness. All this curious tumult within myself was hard enough to bear, I often thought, without the suddenly discovered terrors of the Peters pasture at nightfall, terrors which were increased a thousandfold by the dreadful knowledge that I could not reveal them to anyone.

In our family, as in most well-ordered country families

of the time, a job was a job, to be performed cheerfully and well, whatever its nature. My father hated complaints of any sort; and we children were brought up, perhaps a bit ruthlessly, to keep all minor troubles to ourselves. If I had told him that the Peters pasture beyond its bars was the most frightening place I at that time knew, he would doubtless have suggested that one of my sisters go with me on my journey after Constancy; but to admit my fears was unthinkable, for, awful as they were, they were preferable to his disappointment and even possible scorn. He never reprimanded me when Constancy and I were late, for he knew her habits; and once, when I drove her into our barn just as darkness was falling and he saw that I was tearful and that my arms and face were scratched from an encounter with blackberry vines, he gave me a dime to spend as I liked and called Constancy a *plague* and a *pest*. This kindness so unmanned me, I remember, that I dashed to the privy, where I could sob quite undisturbed. I learned, nevertheless, during those summer evenings of 1899 that one endures, no matter at what price, what cannot be cured except at a greater cost; and the Peters pasture was the means to that wholesome, if bitter, lesson.

It was a large pasture and far more heavily wooded than most, a feature which probably accounted for Constancy's sole occupancy of it. Its lower portion near the log fence which surrounded it was swampy and overgrown by thickets of alder and cherry and by tangles of elderberry, sumach, and blackberry. Beyond these the ground sloped sharply upward toward dense clumps of evergreen trees through which the water of Peters brook fell swiftly downward toward the cove below the graveyard. In the morning, when I took down the bars for Constancy to stumble across them, I always wondered how the pasture, now sunny and hospitable, could so change its nature in the late afternoon. But it always did.

I think I feared it most when there was fog. Thunder and lightning held their own dreads; rain was dismal and pitiless; but these at least were tangible in comparison with that gray, clinging mist, which, stealing from the sea during the dog days of August, wrapped the pasture in its dimness. Then the outlines of the trees became lost in a dark, opaque mass; the unseen water of the brook was a rush of ominous sound; the thickets, which Constancy loved and I hated, were wet and still, yet dripping with myriads of ghostly drops. Sometimes in the mist, as I made the intolerable round of her most likely hiding-places, the swift passage of some bird among the underbrush would startle me into panic, the flutter of my heart echoing the fluttering of its wings. Constancy's bell helped little in ascertaining her whereabouts, for I feel sure she had discovered that, if she stood perfectly still, it would not ring. And, indeed, I feared as much as I desired to hear it, for in the fog its somber, mournful tone only added terror to the shadowy, spectral world in which I moved.

When I recall, even now, those haunted twilights, I do not think I could have endured the Peters pasture had it not been for the two Mountain Pastures and the light which they brought to me during a brief fortnight of that same summer. These two pastures really formed the foothills of Blue Hill Mountain, which rose sharply toward the north above our harbor. They were high, sparsely wooded, and cut here and there by small, swift streams, which in the spring became little torrents of water. They were mostly known to us because of the blueberries which grew profusely in their shallow soil and around their many ledges and boulders; but since they lay at a considerable distance from home, they were not so familiar to us as small children. By the time we were ten years old, however, we climbed to their ragged slopes to pick their berries as we looked seaward, for they afforded a wide view of harbor and islands and the open ocean beyond.

In the summer of 1899, when all our elders were talking with excitement of the dawn of a new century, something exciting dawned upon me in the Mountain Pastures. A young man had come that summer to the village to stay at our one hotel or boardinghouse and to paint pictures. His name was Mr. Hall, and he was regarded with much curiosity by most people in our community. Perhaps contempt was mingled with the curiosity, for to spend good time merely at painting pictures seemed to most of our parents a waste of it and a paltry way to get a living, if, indeed, one *could* be got from such an occupation. Mr. Hall also encouraged suspicion, for he said little about himself, where he came from or who he was. He was spoken of generally as "that artist fellow" and not looked upon with favor.

He was tall and thin with long white fingers and a cough. Every morning when the weather was fine he set forth with his easel and his paints and climbed the hill behind the village to the Mountain Pastures. His sojourn coincided with the August blueberry season, when a large number of children went also to the pastures to harvest their crop of berries. We were fascinated by his presence there and spent as much time as we dared in standing in a silent circle about him, watching him set up his easel and his folding stool, begin to squeeze his paints from little tubes, and mix them on the piece of board which he held between the thumb and forefinger of his left hand. He said very little to us, but he never seemed to mind our standing there.

I picked few berries during that fortnight, for after the others had gone with their pails in search of the best patches, I lingered by Mr. Hall in awe and wonder. I had never seen anyone paint real pictures before or even been clearly aware that they did so. In our village school of that time there were no drawing lessons, and to paint a picture meant only amusing oneself with colored chalks or crayons. Pictures themselves to me had meant little or nothing. The illustrations in books were usually only annoying since they never portrayed the characters as I saw them in my imagination; and as for other pictures, I knew well only those hanging on our walls. These included a portrait of Daniel Webster, purchased by my grandfather at the height of Webster's fame; drawings of the departure of the Pilgrim Fathers and of the signing of the pact in the cabin of the *Mayflower;* a large lithograph of the United States Senate in 1851; and, in contrast, a rather captivating picture in our spare room, of a girl ferrying a boat across a stream, entitled *La Fille du Passeur*, which, my father explained, was French and meant "the ferryman's daughter." In addition to these, there hung also in our spare room two small paintings in gilt frames of my father's little sisters, who had died at six and four years and who wore white pantalettes beneath low-necked pink and blue frocks. I was far more impressed by their early deaths and their odd costumes than by their portraits.

But now here in our Mountain Pastures I saw pictures born on clean white canvas, made by the delicate strokes of tiny brushes, pictures of common things which before I had not thought of as especially noteworthy. I sat for hours on a nearby rock and watched these things come to new life: a clump of white birches with sunlight somehow miraculously streaming across their trunks; clouds which seemed to move above islands in blue water; a heap of gray rocks with the red berries of some elder bushes against them. I often felt an odd sense of embarrassment as I watched Mr. Hall's scanning, careful eyes and his quick fingers, as though I were intruding into a place where he lived alone and where everyone else was unwelcome and unwanted; but I could not make myself go away, counting the disappointment and reproof of my mother over my unfilled berry pail as little in comparison with this wonder.

Mr. Hall rarely spoke to me, and I suppose his usual unbroken silence made some words of his on his last day among us especially memorable. This was the morning when he had painted the red elderberries against the gray rocks. He told me that he was going away the next morning; and then he said most politely:

"Thank you for liking my pictures. Maybe you will paint, too, someday."

Perhaps it was his quiet assumption that I, barefooted and in blue gingham, could ever perform such miracles which emboldened my confidence, for I told him shyly that my dream was to write books when I grew up.

I remember how he looked at me then with amused kindness and yet with a sadness in his face before he gathered up his things and started down the pasture slope.

"I'm sure you will," he said. "And better luck to you than *I've* ever known."

The Mountain Pastures were different after he had gone, filled with new lights and colors. I missed him sorely; and when a year or two later we heard that he had died, I grieved deeply, though in secret. Even now I never see red elderberries against a gray stone wall without a sudden grateful stirring within me.

WORDS

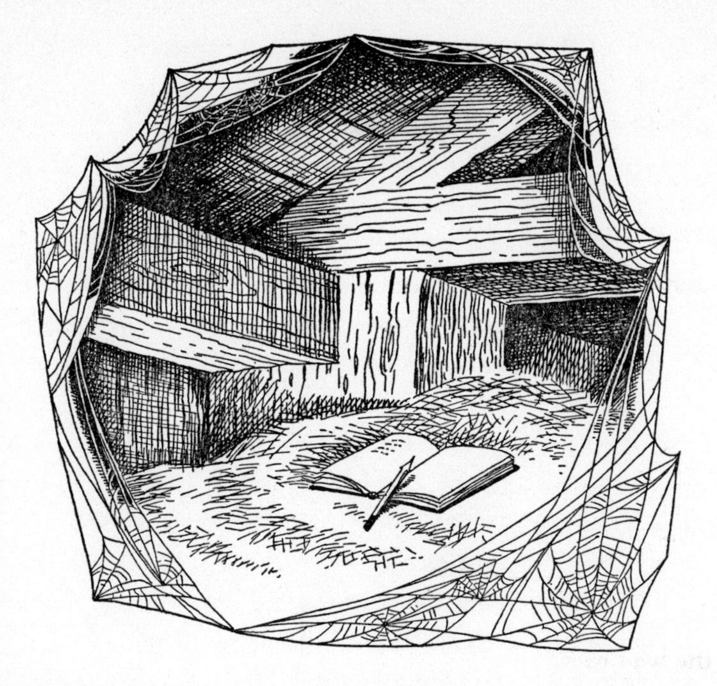

A FEW weeks ago a colleague of mine at Smith College told me a story about his childhood which has ever since made me guilty of the sin of envy. We had been talking about the discovery of words as entities and the sudden, awesome attraction which they often exert over book-loving children early in life. He dated his passion for words before he was ten years old, being more sure of the time of his actual discovery than I of mine because of a gift on his tenth birthday. He said that on that day he was given a little iron safe, complete with a key and a combination which, once learned, opened its door. It was, of course, designed for his pocket money and other small valuables. Instead, having fallen in love with words, he used the safe as a repository for those especially dear to him. These he wrote on small slips of pink paper and placed in his safe, drawing them out often to look at each and to say it over to himself. This safe with its measureless resources was the most cherished of his possessions as a child; and, with the glow of my own early passion still warm and bright within me, I can well believe the truth of his statement.

I am not so certain of the time of my own discovery of single words, their form, sound, and charm, perhaps because I had no little iron safe; but I think that I, also, was well on the way to it by my tenth year. I can, however, clearly trace certain earlier activities and experiences which must have been milestones along the way toward my exciting destination. The first of these activities took place at our dining-room table on many rainy or snowy afternoons and owed its being solely to my mother's powers of invention.

I was not yet of school age when I, together with my two sisters, spent hours at my mother's game of *playing authors;* but I knew my letters, having learned them very early, as children then did, from blocks and from those alphabetical books of glazed canvas familiar to our time. My mother's invention had nothing to do with the real game of *Authors* which we were to play later, sitting with cards in our hands and asking one another, "Have you *Martin Chuzzlewit?*" "Have you *Vanity Fair?*" Hers, like her elevation of us to the top of the old secretary, was yet another means of keeping us occupied and quiet, and it worked admirably. It involved a five-cent copybook for each of us, a pencil, and some book with clear type which we were to pretend to write by printing its words in awkward capitals on the clean paper of our copybooks. I was around five years old when I was encouraged to pretend that I was Charles Dickens and that I was writing a book called *Great Expectations.* My mother always inspected our printing carefully and pointed out the more simple words which we were laboriously setting down. I do not recall that I proceeded very far with my impersonation of Dickens; but I do distinctly remember that I was terrified when I recognized for myself that my sprawling letters spelled:

DONT CUT MY THROAT, SIR. PRAY DONT DO IT, SIR.

My mother's talents for thinking up pastimes to curb and satisfy restless children bore fruit when at six years old I entered the village school, for by that time I could read quite fluently. Indeed, my first day at school marked one of the few triumphs of my entire life, and every detail of that triumph is etched sharply on my memory.

Our village schoolhouse consisted of two rooms, which held respectively the lower and the upper school, or the primary and the grammar. On the September morning when I began my formal education I went, of course, with all the younger children into the lower room with my new slate and my new pencil box and with that vast excitement which rescues, in most minds, at least one day in childhood from oblivion. My triumph began when my teacher discovered early that first morning that I could read, and thereupon wrote a note to the teacher upstairs which suggested that I take my reading lesson with the older children.

I myself bore the note. I still remember every frightened lift of my feet, every throb of my heart, as I went up the dusty winding staircase to that upper room, knocked at the door, walked down the aisle in my blue gingham pinafore, and gave the note to the teacher of the upper school. She received me kindly and placed me, consumed by pride and shyness, at the end of a long settee, which was soon filled with ten-year-old scholars about to begin a Fifth Reader, compiled by a certain Mr. T. W. Harvey. I continued with Mr. Harvey for seven or eight years, there being either no sufficient reason or no sufficient school funds for any change. Together with much dross his Reader contained much gold, and I memorized all manner of each from *The Burial of Moses* and *Somebody's Darling* to *Selections from Shakespeare* and *God's Words to Job Out of the Whirlwind*. I loved every moment of our reading lessons, but I think it was the swing of the lines, the rhythm, and the drama which appealed to me then rather than any magic latent in single words. And I am sure no overworked teacher pointed out that magic to me, even had she discerned it for herself.

I am convinced that the preoccupation with spelling, common to every country school in those years, was a potent influence, however unconscious we were of it at the time, in giving children a sense of words as something more than the correct placing of letters. To fail in spelling was literally a disgrace both in school and at home; and my mother guarded against this humiliation by drilling us in our daily lists of words each morning before we set forth for school. Her very way of pronouncing these as though she cared for them made an impression on me years before they became my own. My uncle Henery's experiments in diction doubtless had their effects also, inseparable as these were from laughter; and I early treasured two words which my aunt Cad was responsible for lodging in my mind. One of these was *monotonous* and the other *weird*. Aunt Cad said that the reiterative sound of the sawmill throughout one entire morning became *monotonous* to her and that a certain misty twilight with a rising moon seemed very *weird*. I asked her what these words meant, and once she had explained them, I made them my own and used each with great pride and no little affectation.

But as I look back upon these early apprehensions of language and try to discern those influences which at last revealed words to me *as* words, quite apart from the stories which they recorded or the lines of poetry which they made to echo in my mind, I incline to think that hours in church were largely responsible for the fascination which by the age of eleven they had come to hold for me. During my entire childhood we submitted every Sunday morning to the reading, long prayer, and longer sermon of an old pastor, the Reverend Ebenezer Bean, toward whom we were early taught to accord deep respect and reverence. His sermons and prayers meant little to me beyond the necessity of sitting still and keeping my head bowed; but I loved to hear him read the Bible. He did this slowly, solemnly, making each word to sound clearly in the stillness of the church; and as I listened, the words seemed to separate themselves both from the page and from his voice until I saw their letters take shape and form, as did those written on the wall with the fingers of a man's hand at Belshazzar's wicked feast. Certain passages, whenever I hear or read them, are still associated with the sunlight streaming through the windows of our church and lying in transparent squares across the pulpit steps, and with the stirring of the wind over the grassy fields outside.

And the twelve gates were twelve pearls; every several gate was of one pearl; and the street of the city was pure gold, as it were transparent glass.

The wind bloweth where it listeth, and thou hearest the sound thereof, but canst not tell whence it cometh, and whither it goeth.

Shortly after my twelfth birthday I began my collection of words. With ten cents of the new half dollar which my grandmother had given me as a birthday gift, I purchased a small copybook, bound in red boards instead of paper and filled with blue-lined white pages. Relieved that I had been able to buy it unattended and unnoted by any member of my family, I took it to the barn loft and seriously considered the surest way of keeping my secret to myself.

My fears of discovery and of mocking disclosure had sound basis. In our house, large as it was, there were few places where one could hide cherished personal treasures with any measure of confidence. Single rooms for the children of large families were virtually unknown, for even if there were unoccupied rooms, few parents of the time saw good and sufficient reason for such use of them. Moreover, any ethical or even humane standards were then, as always, sadly lacking in the normal attitude of one child toward the inner life of another. I remembered uncomfortably, as I sat in the hayloft with my new red book, how I had not long before shamelessly read my sister Edith's diary, which she hopefully concealed under her pillow of our common bed. Burning with resentment over some punishment or bitter sense of injury, Edith had written: *I hate my father, and I do not like my mother very much either.* Since my discovery of her entry, I had utterly demolished her peace and security by quoting these words to her whenever we had one of our frequent squabbles and by even threatening to divulge them. What guarantee, then, could *I* have that she would not find and examine my Word Book and justly pay me back with the same sort of coinage?

I finally decided that the only relatively safe place for my book and for its contents, which might well bring forth jeering comments and even revelations at a time when I was becoming peculiarly sensitive to them, was in the loft itself;

and I at once began to search for some hole or cranny in which I might secrete it. With the help of a small ladder I found such a hiding-place in a high corner of the loft just below our dovecote. Here there was a slit between the barn wall and the joist which supported the roof, and to my deep relief this slit entirely concealed my book.

I decided to begin my Word Book by lists or categories of my newly discovered treasures. My first category, I called *Sad Words* and placed within it *if*, *alone*, *stranger*, *solitary*, *desolate*, and *forgotten*. Later, doubtless with the Peters pasture in mind, I added *shadowy* and *twilight*. My section entitled *Glad Words* began with *radiant*, and that on *Frightening Words* with *darkness* and *death*. One memorable rainy afternoon I suddenly perceived that words with long *i*'s in them were filled with light and thereupon wrote down a list of them, beginning with *light* itself.

Whenever I could escape without comment or undue curiosity on the part of the family, which was beginning in general to distress me in many mysterious ways, I climbed to the hayloft and, taking my book from its dusty, chaff-filled hole, either added to its riches or allowed my imagination to conjure up hundreds of kaleidoscopic images suggested by them. The red book was never discovered, and my frequent annoying preoccupation with its contents, outside the hayloft, was doubtless diagnosed and borne with by my parents as merely another painful symptom found in all children on the threshold of adolescence.

15

A ROOM OF MY OWN

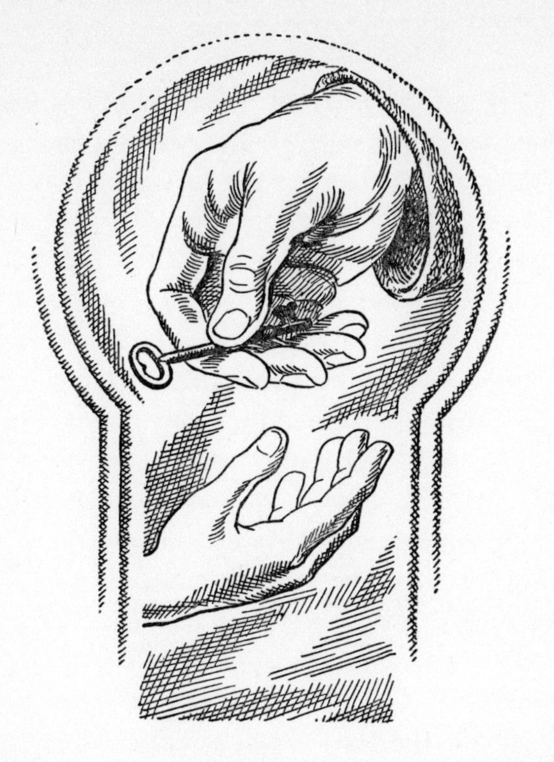

AMONG the many evidences of understanding shown by modern young parents in bringing up their children, none is more wise than the allotment to a child, whenever possible, of a room of his own. True, there are fewer children to the average family than there were sixty years ago; and yet, equally true, there is less space in the average home than in the big houses common to my childhood. I never visit homes of young people today in which each child has his own room, however small, his own four walls within which he may keep his own possessions and treasures, bear his own humiliations and punishments, dream his own dreams, that I do not recall the rooms assigned to most children at the turn of the present century. It was simply taken for granted in those days that children should be bunched together wherever convenient, just as it was taken for granted that double beds were the normal and natural sleeping quarters for them. As soon as one of us children had graduated from our one small bedroom adjoining the big one of our parents, that brief time of privacy, never, of course, appreciated by a very young child, came to an end. At five I was placed with one sister, and later on with both of them, in one large room, and any idea that I, or they, did not necessarily like such an arrangement would never have entered the really considerate minds of my parents. It was as natural and inevitable that children should room and sleep together as that potatoes should be served at every meal or that a family should attend church on every Sunday. And as the years passed and more children arrived within our household, the supply of roommates substantially increased.

From nine years old until twelve I longed for a room of my own, but it never once occurred to me that there was the slightest chance of my having one. A bedroom in my childhood was a place to sleep in, not to escape to or enjoy. It was not even a place to dress or undress in except in spring and summer; and the notion that it might hold other gifts for children than that of mere sleep would have astonished my parents.

I secretly hated sharing a room with my sister, or sisters,

although, on the whole, two roommates were preferable to one since I could have my turn at a bed by myself. I hated it, not because of our one overcrowded closet and our too few bureau drawers, but because of intrusions and discomforts of a far less tangible nature. If I was sent to bed without my supper for some misdemeanor, as I often was, I lay in my half of a big bed, not so much sorry for my sins as aware of the humiliation and embarrassment which I must endure when my self-righteous roommates should later mount the stairs, and either by their contemptuous silence or well-directed words of reproach render complete my degradation. (When they were the culprits, I, of course, was not backward with my revenge.) To share a bed with someone was not conducive either to intimate endearments toward one's doll when one was very young, or to nurturing dreams and fancies when one was older. And if a child perchance loved to make up stories and whisper them half aloud, no place could be less congenial to such an exciting pastime than half a double bed.

In my tenth year the hour of my ultimate salvation began to dawn for me, although it was not until my twelfth that I recognized it as such. When I was ten, my father determined to do away with our necessarily untidy woodshed, which lay between the kitchen and the entrance to the barn. According to his plan, which seemed to my mother dangerously expensive and to us children vastly exciting, we were to utilize our outside icehouse as a woodshed, buy our ice from the town dealer, and convert the space long occupied by our cords of wood and piles of kindling into another downstairs bedroom. This, my father said, could serve my mother as a sewing-room or might ultimately, *when times were better*, house a man who should tend the horses and milk the cow. We called this hypothetical stranger a *coachman* to our awed playmates; but he never evolved.

The room, however, did evolve, complete with a discarded bureau, a washstand, a small table, and a cot bed. My mother rarely used it for her sewing; Annie, when approached, said that nothing could induce her "to sleep so far away from folks"; and the cold, rather cheerless little room remained unoccupied for fully two years. Then, one late September night, when I was driving Constancy home from the Peters pasture, I was suddenly struck by the desperate resolution to ask my father if I might not have it as my own. Even the idea was so revolutionary and unheard-of that I did not dare reflect upon it or postpone its utterance. That very evening when my parents were by some happy chance reading by themselves in the library, I summoned up more courage than I had ever known I possessed, stood before them, and asked for a room of my own.

That they were stunned by my request is an understatement. My mother in particular was overcome, not alone by my question, I feel sure, but also by her genuine concern as to what might conceivably be wrong with me. That a presumably normal and in no way unusual child of hers should of her own free will desire not only a room by herself, but one far away from the companionship and security of the family, was to her both incredible and alarming, and she at once asked me if I had completely lost my senses. My father, who was always more flexible toward innovations of all sorts than was my mother, was more amused than shocked, once he had recovered from his initial surprise. He pointed out carefully in my interest the things which were clearly against such an upheaval of our sleeping quarters, emphasizing especially the isolation of the room and my probable nervousness in being so far away at night; but once I had told him that I had considered these drawbacks (which alas! I had not fully done) and still wanted the room, he looked at me quizzically, yet in a kindly way, said he saw no real reason against it, and returned to his book. After I had thanked him and turned to go, I noticed that my mother had placed her own book on the table and was gazing anxiously from him to me.

The very next day I moved my few possessions into my room. As I did so, the misgivings which had been steadily creeping over me and which were not diminished in power by the dire prophecies of my amazed sisters were stronger within me than was my exultation. Never a courageous child, I was in reality beset by fears. The sudden reminder, as I decided where I would place my bed, which now looked small and cold, that I would some night be awakened by my strange dream became an almost unbearable certainty. More tangible terrors also assailed me. The back window of my room looked out upon thick lilac bushes surrounding our new woodshed; its side window, upon the open fields. Both were low, downstairs windows through which anyone of a marauding nature might peer or even step. The distance between my room and even the kitchen now seemed immeasurable. Although I worked feverishly at setting my things to rights in the hope that activity would quiet my dread, I was tempted by late afternoon to admit my terror and to return, chastened and grateful, to the security of confusion and a double bed. At that eleventh hour, I am sure that pride rather than my desire for privacy (which now seemed feeble and long since past) was all that held me to my decision. Terrifying as were my fears, which were now undermining my resolve and darkening my wish for freedom, even they were more tolerable than confessing them to my father.

He himself, just before I set forth for the Peters pasture after Constancy, restored in some small measure the courage I so desperately wanted. When he came up the road from his office and through the gate, he brought a little three-cornered wall bookcase in his hand, which he said he would screw into the walls of my room once he had finished his chores. But his second bulwark both to my resolve and my security is even more memorable. As he followed me through the doorway of my room and looked upon my furnishings and meager decorations—some cards, picturing roses or lilies, or frosted with country scenes in winter, which I had received for correct spelling in school, tacked to my walls, and a vase of goldenrod, which I had tearfully gathered from the fields—he took from his pocket his ring of keys and separated from it the one which, he said, would lock my door. I had quite forgotten that my room had a key, a distinction unclaimed by any other room in our house. After he had inserted it in the lock of my door and seen that it turned easily, he went away with the smile of the previous evening again on his face. I put the key in the pocket of my dress when I went after Constancy, who for once in her life was mercifully at the pasture bars, nor did I loosen my hold upon it during our slow walk homeward. I had never owned a key before; and in some odd way it slowly revealed itself to me as something more than just the means of locking a door.

When I went to bed that night in my own room with my new bookcase holding my own books on the wall and with my own lamp lighted on my bedside table, I locked my door and put the key under my pillow. My heart was beating furiously, as it continued to do at bedtime for many nights thereafter; and yet I was not too terrified to read for half an hour before I blew out my light. It was the first time I had ever read, alone, in bed, by lamplight. And when I at last knew that I must blow out the friendly lamp and snuggle beneath my covers, my hand happily brushed the wall behind my bed. The wall was warm. I suddenly realized that it was the back wall of our kitchen, which after all was near at hand and in which there would always be red circles of light around the black covers of the Rising Sun, and, in winter, the flame of our lantern on the table.